LITERATURE MADE EASY

ALICE WALKER'S

THE COLOR PURPLE

LITERATURE MADE EASY

ALICE WALKER'S
THE COLOR PURPLE

Written by PAT LEVY
WITH TONY BUZAN

First edition for the United States and Canada published by Barron's Educational Series, Inc., 2002.

Copyright © 2002 U.S. version, Barron's Educational Series, Inc.

First published in the United Kingdom by Hodder & Stoughton Ltd. under the title: *Teach Yourself Literature Guides: A Guide to The Color Purple*

Copyright © 2000 Pat Levy
Introduction Copyright © 2000 Tony Buzan

Cover photograph: A K G London
Mind Maps: Ann Jones
Illustrations: David Ashby

Pat Levy asserts the moral right to be identified as the author of this work.

American text edited by Benjamin Griffith.

All rights reserved.
No part of this book may be reproduced in any form, by photostat, microfilm, xerography, or any other means, or incorporated into any information retrieval system, electronic or mechanical, without the written permission of the copyright owner.

All inquiries should be addressed to:
Barron's Educational Series, Inc.
250 Wireless Boulevard
Hauppauge, New York 11788
http://www.barronseduc.com

International Standard Book No. 0-7641-2064-6

Library of Congress Catalog Card No. 2001 135073

Printed in the United States of America

9 8 7 6 5 4 3 2 1

Contents

How to study	vii
How to use this guide	xv
Key to icons	xvii
Background	1
The story of *The Color Purple*	4
Who's who?	6
• Alice Walker's approach to characterization	6
• Celie: the hard-pressed heroine	7
• Shug Avery: sexy blues singer and law unto herself	8
• Mr._____ (Albert): selfish bully who regrets his mistakes	9
• Sofia: strong woman who runs into trouble with white society	10
• Nettie: Celie's missionary sister	10
• Harpo: Mr._____'s son, Sofia's husband	11
• Mary Agnes (Squeak): Harpo's girlfriend	12
• Alphonso (Fonso) (Pa): exploitative stepfather to Celie and Nettie	12
• Grady: Shug's unworthy boyfriend	13
• Odessa and Jack: Sofia's sister and her husband	13
Themes	17
• Men and women	17
• From ignorance to understanding	18
• Violence	18
• The spiritual world	19
• Slavery and freedom	20
• Love	20
• The bonds between women	21

v

THE COLOR PURPLE

Language, style, and structure	**22**
Commentary	**27**
Topics for discussion and brainstorming	**94**
How to get an "A" in English Literature	**98**
The exam essay	**99**
Model answer and essay plan	**100**
Glossary of literary terms	**105**
Index	**109**

How to Study

You are now in one of the most important educational stages of your life, and the one thing you need even more than subject knowledge is the knowledge of *how* to remember, *how* to comprehend, *how* to study, *how* to take notes, and *how* to organize your thoughts. You need to know how to *think*; you need a basic introduction on how to use that super biocomputer inside your head – your brain.

The following pages contain a gold mine of information on how you can achieve success both in high school and in your college or professional career. These pages will give you skills that will enable you to be successful in *all* your academic pursuits. You will learn:

- how to recall more *while* you are learning.
- how to recall more *after* you have finished a class or a study period.
- how to use special techniques to improve your memory.
- how to use a revolutionary note-taking technique called Mind Maps that will double your memory and help you to write essays and answer exam questions.
- how to zap your reviewing.

How to understand, improve, and master your memory of Literature Made Easy

Your memory really is like a muscle. Don't exercise it and it will grow weaker; *do* exercise it properly and it will grow incredibly more powerful. There are really only four main things you need to understand about your memory in order to increase its power dramatically:

Recall during learning
– THE NEED FOR BREAKS!

When you are studying, your memory can concentrate, understand, and remember well for between 20 and 45 minutes at a time. Then it *needs* a break. If you continue for longer than this without a break, your memory starts to break down. If you study for hours nonstop, you will remember only a fraction of what you have been trying to learn, and you will have wasted hours of valuable time.

So, ideally, *study for less than an hour*, then take a five- to ten-minute break. During this break listen to music, go for a walk, do some exercise, or just daydream. (Daydreaming is a necessary brain-power booster – geniuses do it regularly.) During the break your brain will be sorting out what it has been learning and you will go back to your study with the new information safely stored and organized in your memory banks. We recommend breaks at regular intervals as you work through *Literature Made Easy*. Make sure you take them!

Recall after learning
– THE WAVES OF YOUR MEMORY

What do you think begins to happen to your memory right *after* you have finished learning something? Does it immediately start forgetting? No! Surprisingly, your brain actually *increases* its power and continues remembering. For a short time after your study session, your brain integrates the information, making a more complete picture of everything it has just learned. Only then does the rapid decline in memory begin; as much as 80 percent of what you have learned can be forgotten in a day.

However, if you catch the top of the wave of your memory and briefly review what you have been studying, the memory is imprinted far more strongly and stays at the crest of the wave for a much longer time. To maximize your brain's power to remember, take a few minutes at the end of a day and use a Mind Map to review what you have learned. Then review it at the end of a week, again at the end of a month, and finally a week before your test or exam. That way you'll ride your memory wave all the way to your exam, and beyond!

The memory principle of association

The muscle of your memory becomes stronger when it can **associate**, when it can link things together.

Think about your best friend and all the things your mind *automatically* links with that person. Think about your favorite hobby and all the associations your mind has when you think about that hobby.

When you are studying, use this memory principle to make associations between the elements in your subjects and thus improve both your memory and your chances of success.

The memory principle of imagination

The muscle of your memory will improve significantly if you can produce big images in your mind. Rather than just memorizing the name of a character, imagine that character of the novel or play as if you were a video producer filming that person's life. The same goes for images in poetry.

In *all* your subjects use the **imagination** memory principle.

Throughout this guide you will find special association and imagination techniques (called mnemonics after the Greek goddess Mnemosyne) that will make it much easier for you to remember the topic being discussed. Look for them!

Your new success formula: Mind Maps ®

You have noticed that when people go on vacation or travel, they take maps. Why? To give them a general picture of where they are going, to help them locate places of special interest and importance, to help them find things more easily, and to help them remember distances and locations, and so on.

It is exactly the same with your mind and with study. If you have a "map of the territory" of what you have to learn, then everything is easier. In learning and in study, the Mind Map is that special tool.

As well as helping you with all areas of study, the Mind Map actually *mirrors the way your brain works.* Your Mind Maps can be used for taking notes from your study books, for taking notes in class, for preparing your homework, for presenting your homework, for reviewing your tests, for checking your and your friends' knowledge in any subject, and for *helping you understand anything you learn.* Mind Maps are especially useful in studying literature, as they allow you to map out the whole territory of a novel, play, or poem, giving you an "at-a-glance" snapshot of all the key information you need to know.

The Mind Maps in *Literature Made Easy* use, throughout, **imagination** and **association**. As such, they automatically strengthen your "memory muscle" every time you use them. Throughout this guide you will find Mind Maps that summarize the most important areas of the literature work you are studying. Study these Mind Maps, add some color, personalize them, and then try drawing your own. You will remember them far better! Generally, your Mind Map is highly personal and need not be understandable to any other person. It mirrors *your* brain. Its purpose is to build up your "memory muscle" by creating images that will help you recall instantly the most important points about characters and plot sequences in a work of fiction you are studying.

HOW TO DRAW A MIND MAP

1 First of all, briefly examine the Mind Maps and Mini Mind Maps used in this book. What are the common characteristics? All of them use small pictures or symbols, with words branching out from the illustration.
2 Decide which idea or character in the book you want to illustrate and then draw a picture, starting in the middle of the page so that you have plenty of room to branch out.

HOW TO STUDY

Remember that no one expects a young Rembrandt or Picasso here; artistic ability is not as important as creating an image that you (and you alone) will remember. A round smiling (or sad) face might work as well in your memory as a finished portrait. Use marking pens of different colors to make your Mind Map as vivid and memorable as possible.

3 As your thoughts flow freely, add descriptive words and other ideas that connect to the central image. Print clearly, using one word per line if possible.

4 Further refine your thinking by adding smaller branching lines, containing less important facts and ideas, to connect with the main points.

5 Presto! You have a personal outline of your thoughts and concepts about the characters and the plot of the story. It's not a stodgy formal outline, but a colorful image that will stick in your mind, it is hoped, throughout classroom discussions and final exams.

HOW TO READ A MIND MAP

1 Begin in the center, the focus of your novel, play, or poem.

2 The words/images attached to the center are like chapter headings; read them next.

3 Always read out from the center, in every direction (even on the left-hand side, where you will read from right to left instead of the usual left to right).

USING MIND MAPS

Mind Maps are a versatile tool; use them for taking notes in class or from books, for solving problems, for brainstorming with friends, and for reviewing for exams – their uses are endless! You will find them invaluable for planning essays for coursework and exams. Number your main branches in the order in which you want to use them and off you go – the main headings for your essay are done and all your ideas are logically organized!

HOW TO MAKE STUDY EASY FOR YOUR BRAIN

When you are going somewhere, it is easier to know beforehand where you are going, isn't it? Obviously it is easier if you *do* know. It is the same for your brain and a book. When you get a new book, there are seven things you can do to help your brain get to "know the territory" faster:

1 Scan through the entire book in less than 20 minutes, as you would if you were in a store thinking whether or not to buy it. This gives your brain *control*.
2 Think about what you already know about the subject. You'll often find out it's a lot more than you thought. A good way of doing this is to do a quick Mind Map on *everything you know* after you have skimmed through it.
3 Ask who, what, why, where, when, and how questions about what is in the book. Questions help your brain "fish out" the knowledge.
4 Ask your friends what they know about the subject. This helps them review the knowledge in their own minds, and helps *your* mind get new knowledge about what you are studying.
5 Have another quick speed-read through the book, this time looking for any diagrams, pictures, and illustrations, and also at the beginnings and ends of chapters where most information is contained.
6 If you come across any difficult parts in your book, mark them and *move on*. Your brain *will* be able to solve the problems when you come back to them a bit later – much like saving the difficult parts of a jigsaw puzzle for later. When you have finished the book, quickly review it one more time and then discuss it with friends. This will lodge it permanently in your memory banks.
7 Build up a Mind Map as you study the book. This helps your brain to organize and hold (remember!) information as you study.

Helpful hints for reviewing for exams

◆ To avoid **exam panic** cram at the beginning of your course, not at the end. It takes the same amount of time, so you may as well use it where it is best placed!

HOW TO STUDY

- Use Mind Maps throughout your course, and build a Master Mind Map for each subject, a giant Mind Map that summarizes everything you know about the subject.
- Use memory techniques such as mnemonics (verses or systems for remembering things such as dates and events or lists).
- Get together with one or two friends to review, compare Mind Maps, and discuss topics.

AND FINALLY ...

- *Have fun while you learn* – studies show that those students who enjoy what they are doing understand and remember it more, and generally do better.
- *Use your teachers* as resource centers. Ask them for help with specific topics and with more general advice on how you can improve your all-around performance.
- *Personalize your **Literature Made Easy** guide* by underlining and highlighting, by adding notes and pictures. Allow your brain to have a conversation with it!

Your amazing brain and its amazing cells

Your brain is like a super, *super*, *SUPER* computer. The world's best computers have only a few thousand or hundred thousand computer chips. Your brain has "computer chips" too, and they are called brain cells. Unlike the computer, you do not have only a few thousand computer chips; the number of brain cells in your head is a *million MILLION*!! This means that you are a genius just waiting to discover yourself! All you have to do is learn how to get those brain cells working together, and you'll not only become smarter, you'll have more free time to pursue your other fun activities.

The more you understand your amazing brain, the more it will repay and amaze you!

Apply its power to this *Literature Made Easy* guide!

 (Tony Buzan)

How to Use This Guide

This guide assumes that you have already read *The Color Purple*, although you could read Background and The Story of *The Color Purple* first. It is best to use the guide alongside the novel. You could read the Who's Who? and Themes sections without referring to the novel, but you will get more out of these sections if you do.

The different sections

The Commentary section can be used in a number of ways. One way is to read a chapter or part of a chapter in the novel, and then read the relevant commentary. Continue until you come to a test section, test yourself, then take a break. Or, read the Commentary for a chapter, then read that chapter in the novel, then go back to the Commentary. Find out what works best for you.

Topics for Discussion and Brainstorming sums up the main critical views and interpretations of the novel. Your own response is important, but be aware of these approaches too.

How to Get an "A" in English Literature gives valuable advice on what to look for in a text, and what skills you need to develop in order to achieve your personal best.

The Exam Essay is a useful night-before reminder of how to tackle exam questions, though it will help you more if you also look at it much earlier in the year. Model Answer and Essay Plan gives an example "A"-grade essay and the Mind Map and essay plan used to write it.

The questions

Whenever you come across a question in the guide with a star ✪ in front of it, think about it for a moment. You could make a Mini Mind Map or jot down a few notes to focus your mind. There is not usually a "right" answer to these questions; it is important for you to develop your own opinions if you want to get an "A." The Test Yourself sections are designed to take you about 15–20 minutes each – time well spent. Take a short break after each one.

Themes

A **theme** is an idea explored by an author. Whenever a theme is dealt with in the guide, the appropriate icon is used. This means you can find where a theme is mentioned just by flicking through the book. Try it now!

Men and women From ignorance to understanding

Violence The spiritual world

Slavery and freedom Love

Bonds between women

 LANGUAGE, STYLE, AND STRUCTURE

This heading and icon are used in the Commentary wherever there is a special section on the author's choice of words and imagery as well as the overall plot structure.

BACKGROUND

Walker's life

Alice Walker was born in Georgia in 1944 to a poor farming family. At school she won a scholarship to Spelman College in Atlanta to study literature. For the next 20 years she worked in universities, traveling to Uganda and Kenya in her early twenties and marrying in 1967. She had one daughter. In the 1960s she became involved in the Civil Rights Movement.

Walker's career as a writer began with her first book of poetry. In 1970 she published her first novel, *The Third Life of Grange Copeland*, which concerns itself with relations between men and women. Her second novel, *Meridian*, published in 1976, is based on her experiences with the Civil Rights Movement and was followed in 1982 by *The Color Purple*, which shows the progression of her thoughts from equal rights for all black Americans to the feminism of this novel. Later novels have continued the story of Celie's family, and Walker's latest writing concerns itself with the topic that is mentioned in Nettie's letters – genital mutilation.

The Color Purple was made into a film in 1985, directed by Steven Spielberg, and it provoked much debate about its fairness toward black men. Walker wrote an autobiographical work, *The Same River Twice*, about her experiences collaborating on the movie and the responses to it afterward.

Historical context

The Color Purple begins in the early years of the twentieth century, 50 years after the abolition of slavery in the United States. There were people alive at that time who, like Celie's grandparents, had been slaves. In 1870 all Americans were given the right to vote, and by the time Celie was born, a black person could also own property. But in the deep South these were technical rights only. While Albert's father owned land, Celie's father was lynched along with his brothers for being too successful.

Most black people were desperately poor, and the economy of the South was in ruins, so that even white people had few opportunities in life. The position of women was barely improved from the state of slavery. The slaveholders at least had an incentive to keep them alive – they were valuable property – but their husbands and fathers saw them as drudges and burdens to the family income.

Most black Americans were deeply religious people, often Baptist in affiliation, and the Church would have been a strong element in the lives of most women. In this novel Walker sees the control of the Church as another element keeping women in their place, and she uses the words of Shug, Celie, and Nettie to formulate a new kind of God who allows them the freedom they need.

The story follows the lives of these black women over a period of about 35 years from the early twentieth century to World War II. Characters in the novel seem to become more prosperous as time passes, although there seems to be no improvement in race relations. They are influenced by the Church, and later by the radio, where they hear the music of black musicians such as Bessie Smith and Duke Ellington (both mentioned in the novel). However, the women in this novel seem unmoved by the wars they live through.

The second historical setting is the African one. Nettie goes as a missionary to a country that has actually taken part in the slave trade. It is now being ruthlessly carved up by colonial powers, and during the time she is there she watches the Olinka people's way of life being destroyed by British rubber planters. The novel also reflects the rather arrogant attitude of missionary societies of the late nineteenth and early twentieth centuries, who thought that they could improve the lot of these "simple natives" by replacing their indigenous religions with Christianity.

Political context and the novel's reception

Written in 1982 at a time when black women in America were making great strides in all areas of life, the book and the film that quickly followed it brought huge critical comment from the black community. In an environment where "blaxploitation" movies (which exploited black culture, creating stereotypical black characters purely for profit) such as *Superfly* were

BACKGROUND

coming to an end, this novel and the movie version portrayed black men in many of the stereotypes that had led to lynch mobs and racial discrimination over the previous half century. Sexually voracious, unfeeling, violent, brutal toward women, the men in this novel, according to many critics, damaged the image and the unity of black people and reinforced all the old stereotypes.

The novel was tremendously successful and received the Pulitzer Prize in 1983. The movie was released in 1985 and also received critical acclaim. ✪ What do you think of the claim that the novel creates stereotypically bad male characters?

THE STORY OF THE COLOR PURPLE

From age 14 to 19 Celie lives with her family and, after her mother's death, with Pa's (Alphonso's) new wife. When she is 14, Pa rapes her repeatedly, and she bears him two children, which he takes away from her. After her mother's death, Pa starts to desire her sister Nettie, and Celie offers herself to save her sister the horror of incestuous and brutal rape.

At age 19 **Celie** is given to a local farmer as his wife and begins a life of **abuse** and drudgery in his home. One day she sees a child that she believes is her lost **daughter** and meets the adoptive mother. **Nettie leaves** Pa's house to live with Celie and her husband, **Mr.**_____, until Mr._____ makes sexual advances toward her and Nettie has to run away. Celie advises her to go to the woman she met in town and seek help.

Mr._____'s eldest son **Harpo** marries a strong-willed girl named **Sofia**. Mr._____ advises Harpo to **beat** Sofia as he does Celie. When Harpo tries to do that, Sofia beats him up.

Celie has known for a long time that Mr._____ is in **love** with a beautiful blues singer, **Shug Avery**. Shug falls ill and Mr._____ brings her home. Celie falls in love with Shug Avery and slowly **nurses** her back to health. Celie and Mr._____ find they have something to share in their concern for Shug. Celie discovers that she is sexually attracted to Shug.

Sofia leaves Harpo and takes their children to her sister's house. Harpo turns their house into a **juke joint**. Eventually, Shug goes to **sing** there. Sofia is disrespectful to the Mayor's wife, then **punches** the Mayor and is beaten up and thrown into **prison**.

Shug has **left** Celie and Mr._____'s house and becomes a famous blues singer. One day she comes back to see them. While Mr._____ and **Grady**, Shug's new husband, are out drinking, Shug and Celie discover that there are **letters** from Nettie to Celie going back over 20 years that Mr._____ has kept from her.

THE STORY OF THE COLOR PURPLE

When Nettie left Celie she went to **Corinne**, the woman whom Celie had met, and asked for help. She and her husband **Samuel**, a minister, took Nettie with them and their two adopted children to **Africa**, where they were to be **missionaries**. Nettie's letters describe the **Olinka**, whose ways they try to change until one day a **road** is driven right through their village, destroying their subsistence culture.

As Corinne **is dying** she admits that she thought that Samuel was the children's father and that Nettie was their mother. Nettie discovers that the children were **sold** to Samuel by **Alphonso**, and realizes that they must be Celie's lost children, her nephew and niece. More important, Nettie discovers that Alphonso, the man they called **Pa**, was their stepfather, so the children are not products of incest. Samuel, Nettie, and the children go to **England**, where Samuel and Nettie marry. Then they **return** to Africa.

Shug and Celie discuss **religion** and conclude that God is in **everything** around them and is not just an old white man in churches. They also discover lesbian **sex**. Sofia is allowed to leave the Mayor's house and go **home** to her children. **Mary Agnes** (Squeak) has become a **singer**. Celie decides to **leave** Mr._____. She and Mary Agnes move into Shug's huge house. Discovering a talent for making **pants** (trousers), Celie sets up her own business. She goes back to **visit** Harpo and Sofia and discovers that Mr._____ has taken charge of his house and farm and is doing well.

Alphonso dies and it emerges that Celie and Nettie had owned a **house** and business, kept from them by Alphonso. Then, however, things take a turn for the worse: Shug **goes off** with a young man; a **telegram** arrives to say that Nettie has been killed; and one of Sofia's children becomes very ill.

Celie lives quietly in her house and makes pants. She and Mr._____ become **friends**. **Shug returns** to Celie and Albert. Finally it is revealed that Nettie is **not dead**, when she arrives with Samuel, Celie's children, and Tashi, Adam's wife.

WHO'S WHO?

The Mini Mind Map above summarizes the main characters in *The Color Purple*. When you have read this section, look at the full Mind Map on p. 15, then make a copy of the Mini Mind Map and try to add to it from memory.

Alice Walker's approach to characterization

At the end of *The Color Purple* Alice Walker thanks her characters for appearing to her and calls herself a medium. To Walker these characters are very real people with psychologies of their own, and histories that reveal much about their behavior in the story. Most important, all of them have the capacity to change and learn.

All the characters are shown through Celie's eyes, and it is their language and behavior that make them into real people. As Celie reports whole conversations, we hear Shug's profanities and forthright language, Sofia's straight talking, and Mr.____'s negatives and denials – and eventually his ability to listen and think about his mistakes. Celie's ironic humor starts off hesitantly and grows during the course of her letters, while Nettie remains serious and dedicated to the happiness of others.

But these characters also represent aspects of Walker's viewpoint. While both Shug and Sofia are forthright, Sofia is the more aggressive and more likely to strike out in anger, thus illustrating Walker's point that violence, male or female, doesn't solve any problems. In the same way, Harpo and Sofia are an atypical married couple, she loving physical work and he enjoying housework, making a point about male–female relations.

Celie

As Celie's understanding, humor, and intuition develop, we learn more about her, her family, and the wider society in which she lives. At first the reader has to work hard even to follow what is happening as the confused, terrified child writes to the only one she can ask for help – God. In these early days she has no one she can tell about the shameful thing imposed on her by the man who ought to have been her protector.

As Celie makes friends first with Sofia and then Shug, she gradually recovers. Her wit and sensibilities develop until she can give Harpo and Squeak advice. Her one act of meanness through all the harm done to her is to advise Harpo to beat Sofia, and she quickly regrets it.

Celie's progress is helped by Shug Avery, who offers her a sense of belonging, but, more important, financial independence from Albert. Celie could not have become the woman she is at the end of the novel without Shug's financial help. Other female characters in the novel are constrained by their financial dependence.

In Celie's culture creativity is consistently repressed, whether it is Celie's ability to fashion beautiful clothes or Harpo's love of cooking, Mary Agnes's ability to sing, or Shug's creative sexual energy. Even Albert eventually admits to a love of sewing and he makes a carved frog for Celie. Part of Celie's journey in this novel is the discovery of her self-worth and creativity, which manifests itself in sewing because this was what was available to her.

Celie's physical appearance is another important element in her transformation. Her almost nonexistent sense of self-worth has made her physically ugly, and she remains so thoughout the time she is with Mr._____. Once she leaves him she becomes so physically changed that Mr.____ doesn't even recognize her as she walks past his porch. She dresses in clothes that she makes herself and that suit her – pants and a soft shirt. Interestingly, when the Celie in the Spielberg movie goes to take over her house from Daisy, she is wearing a tight skirt and high heels. The Celie of the novel would never wear these restrictive, sexually alluring clothes – they are part of the Spielberg vision.

Shug Avery

The most complex character in the book, Shug Avery, is Celie's salvation, her educator, her lover, and for a very brief time her rival. Shug's history is almost as wicked as Albert's: She abandons her illegitimate children to her parents; she treats her rival Annie Julia, Mr.____'s first wife, very badly; and she encourages Albert to do the same. When she first meets Celie she treats her cruelly and, worse still, like a servant. Even when she and Celie are together as a couple, she goes off with a young man and leaves her, knowing the hurt she will cause her.

It is Celie's care and devotion that make Shug the generous person she becomes. Like Albert, she has been made cruel by society. In Celie she finds a devotion that she can only compare with her grandmother's love. Her illness is never specified but can be seen as an illness of the soul as much as of the body.

Once she is strong again she seems to bring good wherever she goes, making the juke joint a success, helping Mary Agnes to sing, making Albert promise to stop beating Celie, finding her letters from Nettie, helping her face up to Alphonso, taking her away to Memphis, encouraging her to take on the house and store, and finally teaching her complete self-sufficiency by going away and making Celie realize that she is strong even by herself.

If Shug Avery were a less complex figure, like Samuel, who is all goodness, this would be the stuff of fairy tales, but it is her complexity that makes this story believable. Celie loves her for her wickedness as much as for her goodness.

Shug's role as benefactor is not her only role. She takes part in much of the discussion about the life of the spirit that goes on

WHO'S WHO?

in the novel. Her notion of God is radical but fits in with her lifestyle and with what Alice Walker has to say in this book. She rejects guilt, authority, power, repressed desire, and the established Church, and she worships all physicality, especially sex, whether heterosexual or homosexual. To her, God is a part of everything and praising God is a matter of enjoying everything.

Shug leaves Celie toward the end of the novel and goes off with Germaine, a beautiful 19-year-old man. It is after he has suggested that they visit Shug's children that Shug is finally able to return to Celie and settle down. Meeting her son and getting his forgiveness was perhaps as important to Shug as Mr._____'s apology was to Celie.

Twice in the novel a character suggests that Shug's behavior is masculine because she is direct and honest. But these, Celie comes to realize, are not qualities inherent in men and missing in women; they are qualities that can be enjoyed by those who are free, and Celie, too, is able to become direct and honest as she becomes free.

Mr._____ (Albert)

This is the character who really seemed to take Steven Spielberg's attention. At first he seems another version of Alphonso – brutal, without any consideration for Celie, sexually voracious, utterly selfish, totally uninterested in his children. His history with his first wife is even worse. In addition, he tries to make Harpo's marriage fail by constantly making jibes about his son's inability to bully Sofia. On top of that we learn that, like all bullies, he is a coward at heart, too weak to stand up to his own father.

As the novel progresses, however, we see a different side to Mr.____. He loves Shug Avery desperately and is willing finally to put up with all criticism in order to bring her back to health. We begin to realize that all his viciousness stems from his own disappointment and unhappiness. When he keeps Nettie's letters, he does so out of hurt pride (she has rejected his advances) and jealousy at the relationship between the sisters. Of all the things he does, this, in Celie's opinion, is his biggest crime.

After Celie leaves, he starts to consider his life and gradually comes to acknowledge and regret all his mistakes. He apologizes to Celie about Nettie's letters, makes his peace with her, and comes to realize that he has lost another good woman, perhaps not one he was passionately in love with, but a good, kind friend. His son Harpo comes to love him and so does Sofia, who owes him very little. In the end, his own creativity is stimulated; as a child he had loved to sew with his mother, but this was repressed. Now he carves, and makes shirts.

Albert's repentance and change are a vital part of this novel; without his change of heart this would be a novel about one individual's escape from misery. Albert's change means that change is possible in society, that men need not remain the brutes that Walker depicts, that Alphonso is the exception rather than the rule.

Sofia

Sofia's story takes up the central portion of the novel and is really its greatest tragedy. Sofia represents what happens to women who speak their feelings directly and fight for their rights. Sofia can survive in the black world, as she does when Mr.____ tries to stop Harpo from marrying her, and for a time afterward when she has left Harpo. But confronted by the might of white racial abuse, she tries to take it on and is almost killed for her trouble. She has to become self-effacing like Celie in order to survive.

Perhaps the message of Sofia's story is that fighting always brings suffering and that it is better to turn away completely, just as Celie walks away from Mr.____ and Shug walks away from her family. Later the issue of white racism is settled for Sofia, at least on a personal level, as Eleanor Jane learns about Sofia's treatment and forges a more honest link with her than that of servant and mistress. Walker is saying that white people, too, can learn.

Nettie

In a way, Nettie is a less sharply drawn character than any of the family in America. Her letters remain like travelogues, and a crucial part of the information about Africa that Alice Walker wants to describe – the story of the white Africans (Letter 87) – is actually told by Celie to Albert in order to make it more personal and lively. We suffer with Celie, because of the immediacy of the writing, and enjoy her conversations with her friends, often given verbatim. But from Nettie everything is more distant, written perhaps long after it has happened, and planned like an essay.

Nettie's letters often feel like Victorian **melodrama** (sensational drama appealing to the emotions), because she seems to lack a sense of humor. Her story, too, is more melodramatic than Celie's, with misunderstandings, deathbed forgiveness, a sudden falling in love, and a young girl running off into the bush to be rescued by a lover who suddenly realizes the error of his ways. Her role in the novel is to observe the parallels between Olinka society and Celie's community, and the most successful parts of her letters are her descriptions of the slow destruction of Olinka society. Her letters are less successful in creating a sense of who she is.

Harpo

Harpo is a gentle, kind man to whom Celie responds even in the early days of living at Mr.____'s house. Somehow he is attracted to an unusually forward, strong woman, Sofia, who makes it clear from the start that she will do whatever she chooses and that Harpo is welcome to come along with her. But browbeaten by his father, he first abandons Sofia and then tries to bend her to his will, with comic results. Like his father before him, he is unable to appreciate what he has, and he loses Sofia, indirectly contributing to her terrible treatment at the hands of the white people.

He manages to turn his loss to good, though, and opens the juke joint, finds an amenable, subservient girlfriend, and seems at first to be unhurt by the damage he has done. But eventually even Mary Agnes leaves him and he is reconciled with Sofia, accepting all her decisions with love. He represents another male type – the gentler, more creative man made unhappy by his perceived need to take on a role that doesn't suit him. We never hear from Harpo about any sense of repentance, but we have to take Sofia's word for it when she says she begins to love him again.

Mary Agnes (Squeak)

Squeak's is the more traditional kind of relationship with a man for this society. She has chosen Harpo as her man and, while she reminds Celie of herself, she also feels she has certain rights over Harpo, one of which is not to have him dancing with another woman, particularly his estranged wife. This is the kind of competitive jealousy that Shug was expecting and felt toward Celie when she first came to Mr._____'s house.

Squeak grows in strength as she puts herself in harm's way for Sofia's sake and then takes off to become a singer. Having found her own form of freedom, Mary Agnes can return to her daughter and to Celie's family. Squeak's jealousy over Sofia is mirrored in the stories of the Olinka women who, when a child falls ill, blame each other and make accusations of witchcraft.

Alphonso (Fonso) (Pa)

The most despicable and unrepentant of Alice Walker's characters, Alphonso moves in on a mentally fragile woman and her two children. His voracious sexuality leads him to rape his teenage stepdaughter and keep his wife pregnant until she dies. When she dies he keeps her property, never telling her daughters about their inheritance. He obviously has a tendency to pedophilia since both his next two wives are mere children and his appetite stretches beyond the next wife and Celie to include Nettie. He gives Celie into a life of slavery when she becomes too old and an inconvenience – his wife has discovered what he is doing – and keeps Nettie at home, presumably to satisfy his sexual appetite at a later stage.

Alphonso is intelligent enough to buy the white community's tolerance, making sure that the men who might lynch him are paid off. A sound businessman, he makes his fortune from his stepdaughters' property and dies a happy, fulfilled man mourned by the community. He seems genuinely grief-stricken over the death of Celie's mother and very affectionate to his last wife Daisy. When he speaks to Celie many years later, he tells her that he kept the story of her parentage from her because it was what any good man would do.

WHO'S WHO?

There is a horrific rationality to this man. He seems to believe in his own virtue and has convinced the world around him of it. Like a psychopath he has built up a belief system that permits his terrible behavior. In his world Celie and Nettie – in fact all women under his control – are his to do with as he wishes. To him the house and store are not Celie's because she is a chattel who cannot own land. He believes he was kind to look after children who weren't his and even find a home for a "spoiled" ugly one (Celie).

Alphonso's rationale finds a parallel in the entire white community; they consider themselves better than the blacks, who are, in the white people's eyes, mere chattel. Like Alphonso with Celie, they once owned the blacks and can still treat them any way they wish, hence Sofia's treatment, sanctioned by the entire white community.

Strangely, though, in this moral tale Alphonso never gets his comeuppance. His life is a success, he never faces up to the crimes he has committed, and he dies happy. Even his wife comes out of the marriage wealthy.

Grady

Like Mr.____'s two sisters, who turn up in one letter and never reappear, Grady is a stock figure, necessary for a plot movement or two, an insensitive, sexually promiscuous man who, as Shug says, has two topics of interest – cars and marijuana. He looks good but is never taken seriously by Shug or Celie. His one comment, in Letter 74, *A woman can't git a man if peoples talk*, reduces all the women in the room to fits of laughter. It represents an unreconstructed male attitude that all these women who have suffered so badly at the hands of men find foolish. He disappears by the end of the novel, having caused no real harm or done any good.

Odessa and Jack

These people rarely have much to say in the novel but are responsible for much of the good in it. It is Odessa who takes Sofia in when Harpo abandons her with her first baby and again when she leaves Harpo. Odessa looks after Sofia's children while she is in jail and takes her in when she is

THE COLOR PURPLE

released. Jack figures even less than Odessa but is an unusual man for this society. He takes in his nieces and nephews and provides a home for Sofia when she needs it. Without these good people to help Sofia, there would have been no happy ending for her. Jack is honored in the novel by getting a special pair of pants made for him, and we get our strongest sense of his gentleness from Celie's description of the pants.

Over to you!

? Find descriptions of the pants that Celie makes for her friends and say how they reflect their characters. You may want to make this exercise into a Mind Map, drawing each pair of pants and relating each description to each character.

WHO'S WHO?

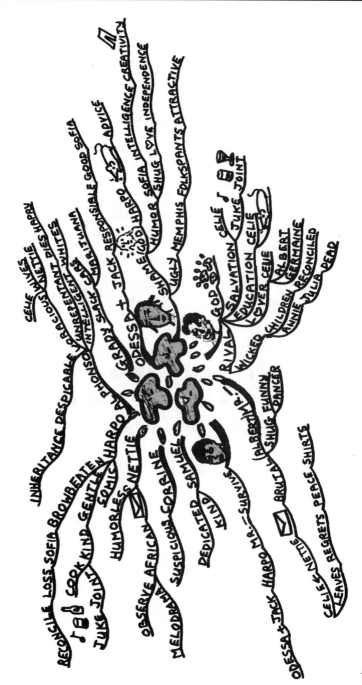

THE COLOR PURPLE

A mnemonic

Remembering all the minor characters in this story can be difficult. Albert (Mr.____) has a first wife, Annie Julia; Alphonso has two wives after Celie's mother, May Ellen and Daisy; and Harpo has two women – Sofia and Mary Agnes, better known as Squeak. There are also Grady and Germaine – Shug's lovers, and Odessa and Jack – Sofia's sister and her husband. One way of remembering the names is to make up mnemonics. Try this one:

Shug *grades Germ*ans	(Shug, Grady, Germaine)
Mr.____ *always judges*	(Mr.____, Annie Julia)
Nettie *samples com*	(Nettie, Samuel, Corrine)
Harpo *married again*	(Harpo, Mary Agnes)
Alphonso *may el*ope	(Alphonso, May Ellen)

Make up lines for Sofia, Odessa and Jack, Olivia, Adam and Tashi, and Alphonso and Daisy. (How about Alphonso's pushing up daisies?!)

Now take a break before looking at the themes of the novel. Think about what kind of pants Celie would make for you.

THEMES

A theme is an idea that runs through a work and that is explored and developed along the way. The Mini Mind Map above shows the main themes of *The Color Purple*. Test yourself by copying it, adding to it, and then comparing your results with the version on p. 25.

The themes below represent one way of looking at the novel, but others can be identified. Patriarchy lies behind much of what Walker wants to say about Celie's life and the lives of the Olinka and all black Americans. Feminism dominates Walker's viewpoint and her treatment of the relationships between women, and the way they leave the men in their lives and eventually return to them. Race relations is another strong theme, especially in the sections dealing with Sofia.

Men and women

Central to this story is the way that male–female relationships in marriage, friendship, and parenthood damage the women and to some extent the men who take part in them. Most relationships in the novel are founded on the fact that men think they are superior to women and have a right to control them, as well as their shared children. Mr.____ makes Celie's life a misery. His father ruins his life and perhaps Shug Avery's too. Harpo ruins a happy marriage with his comical need to dominate. Grady might ruin Shug's life but is too unimportant to her to have any lasting effect. Alphonso lives his whole life at the expense of the women he takes up with.

Evolving in this novel is a new way for men and women to relate to one another. The women find strength from the support and love of their women friends, and finally Harpo and Mr.____ are able to feed into that network of love and support when they give up the misguided values they were taught and return to their truer selves.

From ignorance to understanding

We see this theme played out in the lives of all the characters. Many of the characters begin their lives ignorant of what they want or what will make them happy. They all seem to accept the values of society despite the fact that their learned behavior does not serve their best interests.

Each character moves from this state of ignorance to a happier, more enlightened state. Celie begins as an utterly ignorant child and learns about life as the novel progresses. Mr.____'s form of ignorance is nastier and causes more harm to others, but even he learns what is important by the end of the novel. Shug also learns how to be happy with her life and her children by the end of the novel. Nettie's letters chart her learning about race relations and men and women in the world beyond Celie's culture. Harpo learns about his real needs and happiness and once he understands what he wants, he is able to make other people happy.

This theme links with the theme of men and women because the learning that many of the characters obtain is about how men and women should behave toward one another. Perhaps the one character who does not move in this way is Sofia, who knew what she wanted from the start.

Violence

Underlying all the events in the novel is the potential for violence, whether committed within a family or by the racist white community. We experience Alphonso's psychotic violence, Albert's casual violence, and Harpo's attempt to use violence against his wife, even though he is happy with her.

Central to the novel is the violence of the white community, seen in the terrible revenge perpetrated against Sofia, first on the street and then during the following 12 years. This includes the "passive" violence whereby blacks are kept under control by the fear of reprisals if they dare to protest.

The violence extends beyond Georgia to the world of the Olinka, where anyone who fails to fit in is expelled and where white exploiters thoughtlessly sweep away Olinka society. The violence lies also in the very distant wars being played out as a background to these people's lives. It is a part of the way that men treat women until the women remove themselves from it and the men learn that it is not necessary. Sofia begins the novel a happy, strong woman, prepared to use violence to protect herself, and ends up gripped by hatred, with murder in her heart.

The spiritual world

An important element in the community in which Celie lives is the Church. Its values are narrow and small-minded. Even Samuel hesitates to step in between husband and wife when Nettie asks him to go to see Celie for her. The Church ignores Celie's condition as a child and drives Shug away because she has broken its rules. Celie writes to God because she has no one else, but she comes to feel that the God she thought she was writing to is just another man. After reading Nettie's letters she learns that the white figures in the Bible are a creation of white men and that the Bible says Jesus had hair like lamb's wool – so he may have been black.

Eventually, with Shug's help, Celie formulates a new God that has no gender and few rules of behavior, except that she should love all creation. It is in this context that we see the significance of the book's title. Shug says *It pisses God off if you walk by the color purple in a field somewhere and don't notice it.* The color purple represents everything that is strong and beautiful in creation and what Shug and Celie's God wants is for everyone to appreciate that beauty.

Slavery and freedom

Parallel with the movement away from ignorance and male brutality toward understanding and independence is the escape from a life of slavery to a state of freedom. Not all the characters in the novel achieve this; in fact, we see the Olinka being dragged down from a state of freedom into a kind of slavery. Sofia, too, is enslaved by the white community but eventually gets free and even forms a working relationship with a member of the white family responsible for her enslavement.

Tied in with this, though, is a problem that Walker never really resolves: the need to be financially independent. The Olinka become slaves because whites take away their means of economic survival. Celie becomes free because she can sell clothes, has a rich friend, and inherits a house and store. Harpo becomes financially independent of his father by opening the juke joint. Celie eventually exploits the skills of two women whom she employs to do the sewing for her while she designs the pants, rather as Mr.____ used Celie's labor while he ran things. Walker doesn't suggest how all the people with little talent and no money can achieve freedom.

Love

Almost all the characters in this novel learn the importance of love in its many manifestations. Celie's new God wants everyone to love what he has made; Celie becomes self-aware and independent thanks to Shug Avery's love. Harpo and Sofia find a special kind of love early on in the novel but lose it, only to regenerate a softer, less aggressive kind in middle age. Mr.____ eventually comes to value the fact that, even if it is now over, he once loved Shug Avery passionately and was loved by her.

Shug equates love of God with the physicality of sex and even Celie says at one stage that she and God *make love real fine these days*. The strength of the love between the two sisters remains through 30 years of separation. Walker distinguishes in the novel between good sex and love. Shug and Celie literally make love together, while Shug enjoys sex with men she doesn't love or even know very well.

The bonds between women

It is the support and friendship that the women bring to each other in this novel that saves them all from a life of degradation. Eventually, even some of the men in the story are brought into this chain of support and love and learning, but this is essentially a feminist, antipatriarchal, antiviolence novel in which all good comes about by the actions of women. This extends to the African letters where Nettie notes that the women support and help the other wives and live practically apart from the men.

We see many examples of the support and help of women in this novel: Celie nurses Shug back to health; Shug liberates Celie; Mr.____'s sisters try to help Celie; Shug helps Mary Agnes sing; Mary Agnes gets Sofia out of jail and looks after her children; Odessa provides a home for Sofia; Celie gives Sofia a job; all of them talk and support one another through the worst of their troubles. When the relationships between women break down, then we see death and unhappiness, as in the troubles of Shug and Annie Julia and those between Corrine and Nettie.

LANGUAGE, STYLE, AND STRUCTURE

Celie is the medium through which we come to know most of the characters in this novel, and it is her simple, humorous, and gentle view of the world that comes across. Her language is necessarily simple throughout the novel, although of course as she learns more, her language acquires some complexity. It is that of the southern states of America and seems to be spoken by both blacks and whites, although there is some specifically black dialect in her writing. Her dialect conveys a sense of everyday life in her community much more forcefully than conventional narrative would.

We are never told what Mr.____'s house looks like, but we know they keep clabber (a kind of yogurt drink) in a safe, that Celie cooks home-cured ham and biscuits, that each of them has a very different skin color – either light, like good furniture, dark like Shug, or yellow like Squeak. Celie's imagery is all connected with her everyday life, too, and is often deployed in her descriptions of Shug Avery. Here is her first description of Shug:

> *... she dress to kill. She got on a red wool dress and chestful of black beads. A shiny black hat with what look like chickinhawk feathers curve down side one cheek, and she carrying a little snakeskin bag match her shoes.*
>
> *She look so stylish it like the trees all round the house draw themselves up for a better look ...*
>
> *She look like she ain't long for this world but dressed well for the next.*

When it suits her, Celie can be graphic, and even in this extremity there is a sense of humor in the *chestful* of beads and the conceit of being dressed up for the afterlife.

Celie's language is the dialect of the southern United States. Her use of tenses differs from standard English so that she chiefly uses the present simple tense (*he go*, rather than "he went" or "he is going") as well as dropping the subject-verb agreement common to standard English ("he goes"). Other

LANGUAGE, STYLE, AND STRUCTURE

tenses lose part of their standard structure, such as *I been* rather than "I have been." Celie's spelling reflects her lack of education, most amusingly in *two berkulosis*.

Celie's dialect never restricts the things she needs to say, and often her ideas are expressed more graphically because they are in her dialect; for example, in the passage where she describes the countryside around Alphonso's house: *... all along the road there's Easter lilies and jonquils and daffodils and all kinds of little early wildflowers. Then us notice all the birds singing they little cans off, all up and down the hedge.*

In contrast, Nettie's language is highly discursive, using long complex sentences even when she is describing her personal affairs. For example, she describes the Olinkas' food: *It is taking her* [Olivia] *a long time to become used to the food, which is nourishing but, for the most part, indifferently prepared.* In *indifferently prepared* we hear the voice of the pedant, not someone writing to a sister about her meals.

Several metaphors run through the novel and link the sisters' lives. From an early age Celie seems to be sensitive to trees, often saying she feels like wood and that she knows why trees fear man. In Africa the roofleaf takes on a significance both to the Olinka and to Nettie. It supports their existence and like Celie they feel it is a part of God.

Another symbol running through the novel is the creative power of sewing and in particular quiltmaking, a communal activity that represents the unity of the women in this novel. The symbolism of sewing carries on into Celie's new life, when sewing pants – the symbol of maleness – liberates her from Mr.____ and prevents her from killing him. Later Mr.____ also takes up sewing, thereby taking part in the women's sense of community.

The "color purple" also takes on symbolic significance. It is the color of Celie's and Sofia's bruises but it is also the color of royalty and power and is associated with the beauty of the countryside. When Celie makes Sofia pants, she uses purple cloth to express the power and majesty of her friend. When Albert's sister takes Celie to buy a dress, the color she wants is purple, but we are told that Albert would not allow Celie to wear a dress in that color, perhaps because as a chattel Celie has no right to wear such a proud color. It is of course the color of the Suffragettes.

Structurally, the novel follows the tradition of the naive letter writer, like Mark Twain's *Huckleberry Finn* or Henry Fielding's *Tom Jones*. The narrator reports events that we understand, but that he or she often does not. It follows another very traditional format: the Victorian novel where a family is separated, tragedy befalls its members, and eventually through their devotion and trust they are reunited by strange twists of fate – which happens when Nettie arrives at the house where her sister's children live. It includes sudden twists of plot such as Alphonso's death at the right moment, or Corrine's death just in time for Nettie to find a husband, the sudden revelations of the sisters' origins, and the good fortune of Shug becoming famous.

Strangely, though, there is a difference between this plot and the typical melodrama: the villain – Alphonso – is never punished for his misdeeds.

LANGUAGE, STYLE, AND STRUCTURE

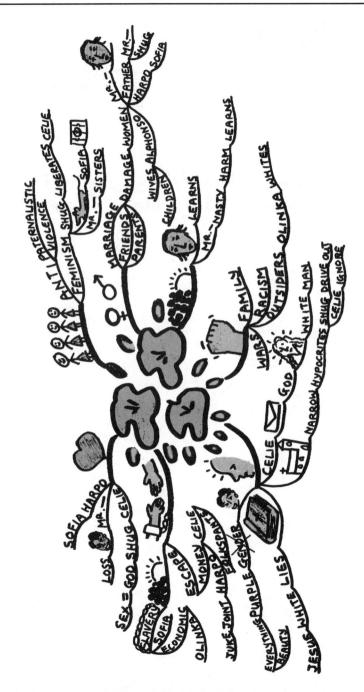

Over to you

? Collect some examples from the novel of the vocabulary and grammar of the southern states. Use it to write an entry in a phrase book for visitors to the area.

Now take a break before beginning the Commentary. Sing your little can off for a while.

Letters 1–8

Letter 1

- ◆ A 14-year-old girl writes a letter to God.
- ◆ She has been told not to reveal a secret or her mother will die.
- ◆ She tells what happened when her mother rejected her father's sexual advances.
- ◆ She gives a naive account of rape by Fonso.
- ◆ She tells God that she feels sick a lot of the time.

The girl has been told that she mustn't tell anyone but God what has happened to her and she takes the threat literally. Until much later in the story our knowledge of the events of Celie's life is arrived at through her letters to God but Celie's God is not a source of spiritual comfort to her. He is just the only one she can tell all this to.

Here we have relations between men and women in this book laid out for us in all their ugliness. Fonso wants sex. He goes to his wife, who denies him it since she is very ill, and so he takes the girl instead. It is clear that he has every intention of using the girl to fulfill his sexual needs indefinitely. ✪ How can we tell this? ✪ At this stage is there any indication of who Fonso is?

We see Celie in her most naive state. She doesn't know why she feels nauseated when she cooks or even have a name for what Fonso did to her. Her feelings of self-worth are so low that she doesn't give us her name. ✪ Why do you think the words "I am" have been crossed out? ✪ How much of what we know about events does Celie tell us and how much do we have to infer from her story?

Letter 2

- ◆ Celie's mother has died.
- ◆ Celie has had one baby and is pregnant with a second.
- ◆ Fonso took her first child, and, she believes, killed it.

THE COLOR PURPLE

Celie's life is a living hell. Fonso uses her for sex and forces her to look after her younger brothers and sisters while she is heavily pregnant, and she has given birth to a child not even knowing she was pregnant. She is used as if she were a slave. Her child has been taken away, and she has no idea what has happened to it.

This novel links the themes of male–female relationships and slavery. Alphonso seems to grieve over the death of his wife. While he treats Celie as something he owns, he seems to recognize certain rules of conduct. ✪ Do you think Alphonso could call himself a good man? ✪ Does he love Celie's mother?

The naive style of the writing is very matter-of-fact and assumes that God knows everything. It gives very little away about how Celie must be feeling. ✪ Why do you think Alice Walker chooses this emotionally restrained tone? ✪ How long do you think has elapsed between the first letter and this one?

Letter 3

- ◆ Celie's second baby has been born, and she thinks Alphonso has sold it.
- ◆ Alphonso is considering Celie's younger sister as the next victim of his sexual appetite.

Celie doesn't question Pa's rights over her and seems even to consider his feelings toward her when she says *He act like he can't stand me no more.* ✪ Why would she act like this? ✪ What does this letter tell us about how Alphonso is dealing with his crimes?

Letter 4

- ◆ Alphonso has married a girl Celie's age.
- ◆ A man who has seen Nettie at church is interested in marrying her.
- ◆ Celie calls Alphonso "Pa" for the first time in this letter.

Alphonso's new wife seems to be suffering. We learn that Albert's wife, Annie Julia, was murdered by her boyfriend

COMMENTARY

as she returned home from church. Celie expresses no horror at the murder or the implied infidelity – she just relates the facts.

What is more important about Nettie's suitor is that he has only three children to look after. Celie wants to make her sister's future life as unlike hers as possible. To Celie men and marriage mean drudgery, abuse, and death. ❂ Do you think she feels sympathy for Alphonso's new wife?

Letter 5

- ◆ Alphonso beats Celie for winking at a boy in church.
- ◆ Celie advises Nettie to marry her admirer.

❂ Why would Alphonso beat Celie for looking at a boy? Celie explains that she is not interested in men. She prefers looking at women because she isn't scared of them. Here for the first time is a brief expression of Celie's feelings: She felt sorry for her mother, who she believes died from trying to believe Alphonso's lies.

Celie's letters to God do not ask for his intervention. She sometimes tells God about events and at other times assumes he knows about them already. We can understand this as a plot device – Celie tells God things that Alice Walker wants us to know, but it is also an essential part of the novel that the young Celie expects nothing from this God, who turns out later to be not only a man but, what's worse, a white man. Eventually she comes to believe that God is not white, male, or all-knowing but a life force that exists in everything.

Things have now come down to Nettie either marrying this man who admires her or the apparently inevitable rape by Pa. Nettie isn't aware of this, although Celie told us in Letter 3 that Nettie was scared. The only possible outcome for the women in this family is marriage and a lifetime of drudgery and pregnancy. Celie at least has the knowledge that she will never be pregnant again; her periods have stopped, probably because she has been permanently damaged by undergoing two pregnancies at an early age.

Letter 6

- ◆ Nettie's suitor, Mr.____, asks Pa if he can have her. Pa refuses.

THE COLOR PURPLE

◆ Celie sees a picture of Shug Avery.

Here we see two men negotiating ownership of women. None of the things most of us might associate with reasons to marry apply here. Pa's objections are practical: Nettie is too young, Mr.____ has too many children. We suspect, though, that he has other motives for not wanting to let Nettie go. What we are hearing is a bargaining process, as if the men were negotiating the sale of a horse.

For the first time a different tone has entered Celie's letters. She has seen the photograph of Shug Avery; Shug is wearing what must seem to Celie symbols of enormous wealth and freedom, looking happy but with a sadness in her eyes. Shug's happiness and power stand in stark contrast to the sale negotiations for Nettie. ✪ Why would Mr.____ be attracted to a woman like Shug Avery when he seems to favor a submissive young girl as a wife?

Letter 7

- ◆ The new mother is sick; Alphonso starts to focus his attentions on Nettie.
- ◆ Celie asks him to spare her sister and take her instead.
- ◆ He offers Celie, her cow, and some linen to Mr.____.

Celie loves her sister and is willing to endure a beating and Pa's sexual appetite in order to protect her. Later when the two men are renegotiating Mr.____'s needs she takes out her picture of Shug and uses it to console herself.

The knowledge Pa forced on Celie at the age of 14 has finally come to the other two teenage girls under Alphonso's control – Nettie and the new mother. In the emotional upheaval created by Alphonso, the three women support and help one another. Alphonso meanwhile sits calmly on the porch discussing the removal of one of his women.

The conversation between Alphonso and Mr.____ is in some ways the lowest point in Celie's life. Their talk is about the transfer of property. Celie's selling points are her infertility, her sexual passivity, her stamina, a cow, and some linen. Her disadvantages are her ugliness, her generosity, and the fact that she isn't pure.

COMMENTARY

Letter 8

- ◆ Mr.____ makes up his mind to accept Celie.
- ◆ Celie thinks back to when she went to school.
- ◆ Celie and Nettie know the importance of learning, and they study hard at home.

Celie, now about 19, knows that Alphonso has his eyes on Nettie, and she hopes Mr.____ will take her too so Nettie can live with her. ✪ What do her dreams of running away tell you about Celie?

The thought of running away from Mr.____ reminds Celie of how important it is to be educated. She and Nettie think that education is facts, like the names of Columbus's ships. Her humorous comment on Columbus's underhandedness in kidnapping Native Americans shows us that under her youthful ignorance is a subtle and intuitive person. ✪ Why do you think Alice Walker chooses this story from American history for Celie and Nettie to be discussing?

Celie's letter flashes back a few years as she tells the story of how she had to leave school. She is 14 and unknowingly pregnant, and Alphonso doesn't tell her, although he realizes it. We hear his views on women like the schoolteacher who speak their minds; they can't get a man because speaking isn't a useful or desirable attribute in a wife. ✪ What qualities in a wife do you think would be useful to a black farmer in America in those days? Which qualities, besides talking, would not be?

Back in the present, Mr.____ shows up and looks Celie over as if she were an animal for sale. He finally agrees to take her only because she has a cow. Celie's feelings on the subject are not sought and she does not report them.
✪ Although these letters are written about events from various times in Celie's past, they are written largely in the present tense. What effect does this have on the reader?

Over to you

? If Alphonso wrote letters to God, what do you think he might put in them? Try writing one for him about these events.

31

THE COLOR PURPLE

> **?** We have seen how this writing is at once naive in style and yet uses techniques very close to the style of writing known as **stream of consciousness**. Draw a Mind Map showing the various threads in Celie's thinking as she writes Letter 8 to God. Compare it with the one printed on the next page and see if they agree.

> **?** Look at the way the language has changed from Letter 1 to Letter 8. Make a note of the changes in style and length that you see in the letters and think about why Alice Walker is making these subtle changes in style.

LANGUAGE, STYLE, AND STRUCTURE

This novel takes a form with a long history in English literature, the **epistolary novel**. In this part of the story the naive Celie is writing her letters to God. Her choice of correspondent is not without meaning. Without rights, threatened by the man she thinks of as her father, confused about right and wrong, she turns to a figure who she believes watches over events in her life and yet takes no part in them. At no time does she seek God's intervention, although she does ask him what is happening to her body during her first pregnancy. He is a distant figure, a man.

The form allows Alice Walker to present her heroine as a developing human being. We are allowed into the secrets of her heart indirectly as we infer from her blunt statements what her life must really be like. At first she is so broken down by her life that she doesn't give us her name. We learn her name almost by accident as she reports Alphonso's conversation with Mr.____.

In these early letters her style is that of a child, with short sentences, much use of Black American English forms, misspellings, and a very limited vocabulary. As the novel progresses her style changes, but Black English remains as the form that the adult, sophisticated Celie chooses to use. Although she doesn't use her own name and avoids using Alphonso's, calling him "he" when she refers to him, she does use the names of those people that she loves – Nettie and Shug Avery. Mr.____ is not named in this part of the novel either, as if naming him would give him more reality in her life. Much later in the novel he becomes Albert.

COMMENTARY

THE COLOR PURPLE

Try this

? Find some examples of Black American English and say how they differ from the more conventional written forms.

? Find examples of the way that Walker presents us with violence in these early letters. Why do you think she doesn't make the violence more graphic?

Take a rest before going on to the next set of letters.

Letters 9–12

Letter 9

- ◆ Celie goes to Mr.____'s house.
- ◆ His son throws a rock at Celie and cuts her head.
- ◆ While Mr.____ is "on top of" her she thinks of Shug Avery.

Celie's first day at Mr.____'s house involves tending to his children and Mr.____ barely registers his son's violence toward Celie. While the little girls cry over their hair combing, Celie registers no emotion. It is a luxury she cannot afford. Like her earlier letters, which relate the most traumatic experiences, this is brief and the bare facts say more than a vivid description could.

Letter 10

- ◆ Celie sees her little girl in town.
- ◆ She talks to the child's mother.

Celie knows instinctively that the 6-year-old girl is hers. Strangely, the woman has somehow realized that the child's name is Olivia. Celie notices, and the mother confirms, that the child has strange, adult eyes. When the woman is humiliated by the white shopkeeper, Celie is moved to comfort her, but to do so would make matters worse. Instead she offers

COMMENTARY

the woman a seat in her wagon while the woman waits for her husband. This is Celie's longest letter so far and is full of love for her daughter and kindness toward the woman.

Relations between blacks and whites underlie much of what happens and contribute to the violence and oppression we encounter in the novel. This is the first time that we see the white world through Celie's eyes. The racist shopkeeper is noted but not judged. Bigotry is just a part of this society and no one questions it, just as Celie doesn't question men's rights over her body and life. Here the Reverend's wife is humiliated in front of the poor black girl and the other white people in the shop.

Letter 11

- ◆ Nettie comes to live with Celie and Mr.____.
- ◆ Mr.____ tries to flirt with her.
- ◆ Finally he says she must leave.
- ◆ Celie tells her sister to go to the Reverend and his wife.
- ◆ Nettie promises to write.

This letter is much more reflective than any of the previous ones. We can see that an adult Celie is emerging, resigned to her life and deeply cynical but with a fine sense of humor. Alphonso has made it necessary for Nettie to leave. She is older than Celie was when he raped her, but still we can see that she is not as passive as her sister. Nettie plans to get help for her younger sisters because she fears what Alphonso will do to them. Celie's feelings emerge in the dark hope of *Maybe kill, I say*.

There follows a long reflective passage on Nettie's good qualities, which begins as a story about Mr.____ coming out onto the porch, and dissolves into a picture of Nettie instead. She works hard, tries to teach Celie about life, teaches her to read and spell, and Celie fears that her only future options are marriage to the likes of Mr.____ or work as a maid or cook for a white family. Nettie knows what Celie's problem is – she won't fight for herself – but Celie says that all she knows how to do is survive.

THE COLOR PURPLE

Mr.____ dresses up to please Nettie and flatters her, and finally when he realizes that she has no interest in him, he says she has to leave. ○ Is there a real difference between Alphonso's attitude to the girls and Mr.____'s or is it just a matter of degree?

Celie gives us a picture of Mr.____ as a father. The children nag at Celie for things and she gives in to them, but when they approach their father he ignores them. However, there is no undertone of violence here, as there is with Alphonso and his sons and daughters. Mr.____ simply isn't interested. Nettie tells Celie that she must fight for her rights in this family. ○ Do you think this is the root of Celie's problem? ○ If she stood up for herself, would all her problems go away?

Celie is quickly maturing into an insightful adult. Whereas in earlier letters she is confused and barely has the words to describe events in the simplest way, now she uses humor to describe her situation. She finds Mr.____'s attempts to impress Nettie amusing and humorously tells us that Nettie flatters her so much that she feels positively beautiful.

Letter 12

- Mr.____'s two sisters come to visit.
- One sister, Kate, returns and insists Celie is bought a dress.
- Kate argues with Mr.____ about the way he treats Celie.
- Celie thinks Nettie is dead.

This letter is interesting because it gives us a third party's view of Celie and her life. We learn that Celie is a good mother to the children, looks after the house well, and is a good cook. We also learn that the previous wife didn't look after her own children as well as Celie does and that Mr.____ married her and left her alone most of the time while he went off with Shug Avery. Mr.____'s sisters approve of Celie as a wife but disapprove of Shug Avery.

Later, on a second visit, one of the sisters insists that Celie is bought a dress and tries to intervene with her brother to improve Celie's life. She fails and returns only to tell Celie that she must fight, just as Nettie did before. Celie is now convinced that Nettie is dead since she hasn't written to her

COMMENTARY

and thinks that if she fights back she will die too. Mr.____'s sisters try at least to provide support and help to Celie, but it is much later, through her relationships with Sofia and Shug, that Celie finds the strength to fight back.

Over to you

? Letter 12 holds the first mention of the "color purple." Celie associates it with Shug Avery. Why do you think that the color is so important in this novel?

? If you have watched the film *The Color Purple*, make a list of all the changes that Steven Spielberg has made to the story so far. Do they indicate a different interpretation of the novel or are they just the way the story has to be presented in cinematic form? The following are some of the additions or changes Spielberg made. Beside each one say how you think it alters the perspective of the novel and why Spielberg added or changed it.

◆ Scene where the early teenage Celie trudges behind Mr.____ on the way to his farm.

◆ Celie and Nettie standing on a swing, reading *Oliver Twist*.

◆ Mr.____ attacking Nettie on her way to school.

◆ Celie reading to herself from *Oliver Twist* as the figure changes from the child actress playing the part of the young Celie to the adult one.

? Make a Mind Map of Celie's life so that each branch represents another aspect of Celie's life. Add to it as Celie's life develops.

? Find six quotes that could be used to illustrate an essay showing how Celie has matured during the course of these letters.

 ## LANGUAGE, STYLE, AND STRUCTURE

In this series of letters we can see the rest of the story emerging. Celie has spotted her baby daughter with a woman, and when Nettie leaves, Celie suggests to her that she find the woman and ask her for help, setting in motion the subplot of Nettie in Africa and the eventual reunion of Celie and her children. Nettie has promised that nothing but death will stop her from writing to Celie, which points the way to the series of letters from Nettie later in the story. Mr.____'s sisters provide a brief external view of this family and especially of Celie. It would be out of character for Celie to tell us what a good job she does with Mr.____'s children so the two sisters appear here but do not return to the story.

Celie's letters are now longer, contain quite subtle ironies, and are much more reflective than the childish early ones. She begins to share her thoughts with God, about how being married to Mr.____ is worse than death, and how fighting for her rights will just get her killed.

Before the next set of letters spend a little time catching up with your own correspondence.

Letters 13–21

Letter 13

- ◆ Harpo asks his father why he beats Celie.
- ◆ Celie tells God about her beatings.
- ◆ Harpo tells Celie about a girl he likes.

We see Mr.____ passing on his worldly wisdom to his son. Harpo asks why he hits Celie. His answer says much about the culture in which he lives: He beats her because she is his wife, because she is stubborn, and because it is all that women are good for. Later in the novel Celie tells us about Sofia's mother and we meet Mr.____'s father, and they fill in the background of a society where men customarily abuse women and children. We recall that Celie sent her sister to the Reverend's wife because she was the only woman Celie had ever seen with money.

The description of Mr.____'s abuse of Celie is restrained and focuses on her response rather than his violence. She makes herself *wood* in order to deaden her feelings and says that she knows that trees are afraid of men. Later in the book this image of trees as feeling creatures is resurrected when Celie and Shug talk about God. In Letter 12 Celie describes the way that Mr.____ looks at her as if he is looking at the earth. Celie seems to feel herself part of nature rather than of human society.

Letter 14

◆ Mr.____ gets ready to hear Shug Avery sing.

Here we see the thoughtless, cruel Mr.____ in a different light. He is nervous, unsure of himself, and foolishly vain to the point that he is pleased by Celie's flattery. He even seems to care enough to lie to Celie about why he is dressing up. We also see the beginnings of love in Celie. She is carrying around a poster that shows Shug Avery dressed in outlandish clothes and with an assertive smile. ✪ Why do you think Celie is so attracted to her?

This passage is one of happiness and humor and is the first one like it in the novel. It marks a change in the relationship between Mr.____ and Celie. Although Mr.____ doesn't know it, they have something in common for the first time – their love for Shug Avery.

Letters 15 and 16

◆ Mr.____ returns from seeing Shug Avery.
◆ He leaves Celie and Harpo to do all the work.

Another view of Mr.____. He is depressed and sits around all day thinking about Shug Avery, leaving Celie and Harpo to do all the work. He seems too distracted to be his usual cruel self but is spiteful enough when Harpo challenges him.

Letter 17

◆ Harpo and Sofia plan to marry.
◆ Sofia visits Mr.____.

Here are several aspects of the relationships between men and women in this community. The normal courting arrangements of young men and women can be seen in the very proper visits by Harpo to Sofia's family. Her father's objections to him reveal much about this community. Harpo's poor prospects and disreputable father mean nothing beside the scandal of his mother's death.

Mr.____'s reactions are in keeping with his contempt for all women as well as his contempt for his own children. His language is ugly and insulting but Harpo keeps silent; he is as intimidated by Mr.____'s violence as Celie is. Mr.____ has assumed that Sofia has come to him out of desperation, that her father has thrown her out of his house, as Mr.____ no doubt would do to one of his own daughters. But he is wrong and Sofia tells him so. He has no power over her and she walks away, leaving Harpo behind.

This new woman in Celie's life is a very different creature from any of the other women she has so far met. She is unafraid of Mr.____ and corrects him when he says she is in trouble. When Mr.____ abuses her, she laughs at him and marches away *like the army change direction and she heading off to catch up*. She is disappointed in Harpo but has the strength to walk away from him.

The love among the family in this story is dead, like a tree made into furniture. Celie admits she looks after the children and gets up in the night to comfort Harpo when he has nightmares, but says it is like patting a piece of wood, like herself. The other children ignore her and do what they want and Mr.____ takes no interest in them. Harpo is the only one with any humanity or love, and that is deliberately erased by Mr.____ when Sofia comes to visit, not because he cares about Harpo but just out of his natural spite. Sofia's family seems little better at first sight, except for her sister, who offers her a home.

Letter 18

- ◆ Harpo and Sofia marry.
- ◆ They move into the little shed on Mr.____'s farm.

Harpo has found the strength to defy his father. His father has agreed to pay him for his work on the farm and has given them a shed to make into their home. ✪ Why do you think Mr.____ has behaved in this generous way? Harpo and Sofia seem very happy and Harpo works hard in his father's fields. Mr.____ doesn't recognize their happiness though. He just sees that Sofia will *switch the traces on you*. ✪ What do you think he means by this?

Letter 19

- ◆ Harpo seeks his father's advice.
- ◆ Celie tells Harpo to beat Sofia.
- ◆ Sofia fights back.

Harpo has become unhappy because Sofia leads an independent life, choosing where to go and what to do. His account of trying to make her do what he says sounds petty; he wants her to stay at home with him but she goes off to her sister's house. Mr.____'s response is to ask how Harpo expects her to do what he says if he never hits her.

So far we have seen a society where women are completely in the power of fathers and husbands. No one seems to question men's right to bully or dominate their wives and daughters, especially not the women. Mr.____'s sisters make little or no effort to help his first wife or Celie. Nettie's only option is to run away from her father, leaving the new mother and the children to Alphonso's mercy. The Reverend's wife has money and so has a little power over her life.

Sofia is the first woman we have seen who does not acknowledge the rights of men over her. Celie tells us that Sofia doesn't stop talking when men walk in the room and that if they ask her where something is, she says she doesn't know. ✪ What would Celie do? Here the worst happens. Celie, out of jealousy at Sofia's independence and the happiness in her marriage, and because she knows Sofia pities her, tells Harpo to hit Sofia. Even Celie, who has suffered the most in this ugly society, wants to restore its norms, to put Sofia in her place.

Violence is an embedded part of life, according to Mr.____. Women, like children, must be beaten so that they will understand their position in life. The way he sees it, it is a man's duty to abuse his wife and children. He tells Harpo that Sofia needs taking down a peg or two. This puts Mr.____'s generosity in bringing Sofia to his farm in a new light.

Harpo takes his father's and Celie's advice seriously because the next time Celie sees him he is battered and bruised. For the first time in this story a woman has fought back against male violence. ✪ Is this what Celie should do to win her independence?

Letter 20

◆ Celie witnesses a fight between Harpo and Sofia.

There follows a rather comic description of the complete ruination of Harpo and Sofia's home while their children quietly make mud pies outside. Sofia wins the fight because after it, they go off to her sister's house anyway, which is presumably what they were fighting over.

Letter 21

◆ Celie makes her peace with Sofia.

Celie begins to have nightmares because she has betrayed Sofia. Eventually, Sofia confronts her about it and the two women begin to tell each other about their lives. Sofia grew up in a family where there was constant danger from her male relatives. She doesn't say what kind of danger but we can guess. Somehow Sofia's character and the support of her sisters has made it possible for her to learn to fight.

We remember that it was her sister who took her in when she was pregnant and we get a picture of a supportive, strong group of women who, with two of their brothers, fought for one another. They discuss the need to fight for any degree of independence or quality of life in their community and Celie admits that in her case anger made her physically ill because the only anger she ever felt was at her parents and she believed that to be wrong. When Sofia tells her she should bash in Mr.____'s head the two women laugh over their situation and begin work on a quilt.

Sofia has adopted male behavior in her attempts to create a meaningful life for herself. When threatened, she literally fights back. She says she loves Harpo but will kill him before she will let him behave like Mr.____ does to Celie. We hear about Sofia's mother, who tried to fight for her children

COMMENTARY

but suffered the worse for it. ✪ Is Sofia's violence a viable option for her and for other women in this society? An interesting point that Sofia makes about her father is that he hates children and *where they came from* – their mother, or, even more significantly, women in general. ✪ Is this a society where for some reason men hate women? ✪ Why would they?

Now try this

? Add the events of these letters to the Mind Map of Celie's life. Is Sofia a new arm of the Map or an extension of an earlier one?

? How many years do you think have elapsed since the letters began? Look back through the text for clues as to how much time has passed. One time marker that Alice Walker gives us is the three years that she says Harpo has been married. Fill in as much of the time chart below as you can. Is there any way of telling in what period of American history this story is taking place? Are there other events that can be located against Celie's age?

Event	Celie's Age
Pregnant. Begins letters	
Married to Mr.____. Harpo age 12	
Harpo age 17 falls in love	
Harpo marries Sofia	
Celie and Sofia talk	

? How far do you agree with the following statements? Score each one 0–5 (0 = totally disagree; 5 = totally agree).

   1 This is a story about an inadequate young woman who cannot stick up for herself. ☐

   2 Celie is so damaged by the things that have happened to her that she can no longer feel. ☐

THE COLOR PURPLE

3 Mr.____ just needs someone to show him that he can't behave like that and he will become a nicer person. ❏

4 Sofia represents the only way to deal with the men in this society. ❏

5 The women are just as much to blame for what is wrong as the men. ❏

6 Black men in this society are angry about the way they are treated by whites and so they take it out on the women. ❏

7 Freedom and quality of life have little to do with economic independence; they are a state of mind. ❏

? Start a Mind Map of Sofia's character. Each branch could give one adjective to describe her; further branches could be key words for events that have happened to her.

? What things do Celie and Sofia have in common? Make a Mind Map of them. Make a second Mind Map of their differences. Which is bigger?

Letters 22–27

Letter 22

- ◆ News comes to town that Shug Avery is sick.
- ◆ Mr.____ goes off in the wagon and brings Shug back to his house.
- ◆ As they carry the very sick Shug into the house she laughs at Celie's ugliness.

We get a glimpse of the wider black community, in particular the church that Celie attends. Shug's illness is generally considered retribution for her evil ways. The sermon is about wicked women who have the temerity to smoke, drink, wear sexy clothes, and sing for money. Going off with married men comes a long way down the list of sins. Celie is becoming aware of the hypocrisy of this community that

COMMENTARY

tolerated without question two teenage pregnancies and a forced marriage, and that presumably tolerates wife beating, abandonment, child abuse, and laziness on the part of its men.

We learn that besides her chores at the farm, doing the housework, looking after the children (who by now must be in their teens), and looking after the crops, Celie also does much of the work for the church. ✪ Why do you think she does this since it is voluntary? ✪ What do you think she thinks of the preacher after his sermon?

This letter also reveals much about Mr.____. He doesn't have the courage to defend Shug Avery in public, revealing that like all bullies he is a coward at heart, but afterward he rides off to get her. He loves Shug so much and Celie means so little to him that he is halfway through the door of the house with Shug before he even thinks of telling Celie who she is. But strangely, even then he avoids the whole truth. ✪ Why does he pretend to Celie that Shug is just an old friend?

💗 As soon as Celie realizes that Shug Avery is in the wagon, she behaves just like Mr.____ did when he was getting ready to hear Shug sing. She is frozen to the spot and tries to improve her appearance as quickly as she can. Her description of Shug is an act of love. Even when Shug insults her at a moment when by most people's reasoning she should be most humiliated – her husband bringing his lover into the house – Celie admires Shug for her "meanness."

Letter 23

- ◆ Shug starts to recover a little.
- ◆ Celie asks Mr.____ what happened to Shug.

💗 Celie begins to learn about Mr.____. She remembers that his name is Albert and notices that he has a weak chin and that Shug Avery has total control over his actions. Shug and Mr.____ were prevented from marrying by his father, which puts Mr.____'s behavior over Harpo and Sofia's marriage in a new light and confirms his cowardice.

Celie begins to see Mr.____ as a frail human being rather than something that makes her feel "like wood." Mr.____'s tears seem more like self-pity, though, than grief for his lover. ✪ When Shug says *no weak little boy can't say no to his daddy*,

THE COLOR PURPLE

what do you think she means? ✪ If she and Mr.____ had married, would they have been happy?

This letter explains much of Mr.____'s ugly nature toward his wives and children and reveals much about Shug Avery too. Celie delights in Shug's viciousness, even when it is aimed at her, and is amazed at how timid and humble Mr.____ is when he is with Shug. Celie says that Shug is very ill but her evil is keeping her alive.

Letter 24

◆ Celie and Shug talk for the first time.

At first Shug is very hostile to Celie. ✪ Why would she be like this? Celie must look a little strange to her, gazing at her naked body and almost obsequious when she could be expected to be resentful of Shug's presence in the house. Shug is not the least bit grateful to Celie and acts as if she is in the presence of a fool. Celie, meanwhile, is trying to deal with her sexual attraction, which she doesn't understand. The two women find a little common ground in their children. Celie has lost her children and Shug has walked away from hers.

So far in the novel we have seen little evidence of any sense of spirituality. Celie's religion has been a purely practical thing. God is the only one she has to write to and heaven is the place where she will go when her suffering on earth is over. Several times she has referred to trees as if she identifies more with the earth than with God. Here, when she washes Shug's body, she says it feels like praying.

As Celie learns more about the world, she is able to describe it and understand it more fully, until now she is far beyond the petty jealousies of the churchwomen and can see just what a weak, silly man she has been terrified of all these years. Here she is learning about her own sexuality for the first time and although she doesn't have a name for what she feels, she considers it to be good, like a religious experience.

Letter 25

◆ Celie persuades Shug to eat.

COMMENTARY

Shug accepts Celie's service and although she is still full of viciousness, she tolerates her presence. Celie fluctuates between her sexual desire for Shug and seeing Shug as a bad-tempered child who isn't getting her own way.

Celie's love for Shug is different from Mr.____'s. All Mr.____ can do is watch Shug. His love finds no practical expression. He doesn't understand how Celie persuaded Shug to eat. Her explanation makes Mr.____ laugh out loud in relief.

Celie shows her depth of understanding of human nature and her subtlety. She even begins to share her understanding and humor with Mr.____. She can look at Shug and see the dissatisfaction in her soul as she flicks through a magazine full of white women, and understands that Shug is too proud to admit she needs help.

Letter 26

◆ Celie combs Shug's hair and listens to her sing.

A brief letter, full of love, about combing Shug's hair. Finally all the resentment and anger against Celie has left Shug, who tells Celie that having her hair combed reminds her of her grandmother. Celie in turn is put in mind of the people she used to love: her baby Olivia and her mother. ✪ How do you think Mr.____ understands the friendship developing between Celie and Shug?

Letter 27

◆ Mr.____'s father visits and threatens Mr.____.
◆ Mr.____'s brother Tobias visits.

Here we see the cause of all the hatred and anger in Mr.____'s life and we realize that it wasn't Celie or his children that he was angry at, but his own father. This old man stopped Mr.____ from marrying Shug Avery when he had the opportunity by intimidating him just as Mr.____ did his own son Harpo. This time the old man comes to abuse Shug. She is ugly, he says, listing her shortcomings, and when that fails to impress, he insinuates that she has a venereal disease. Then he throws doubt on her parentage and that of her children – truly hypocritical criticisms in the light of his own son's conduct.

He is followed some time later by Mr.____'s brother Tobias, another ugly character who hopes to stir things up. Tobias tries to do this by flattering Celie, trying to create the disharmony he was hoping to find. Instead he creates a sense of unity among the three others. For the first time in her life, Celie feels as if she is in the right place.

Here we see Celie at her nearest to violence so far. She spits in the old man's drinking water and considers adding first powdered glass and then urine. The worst of her anger is humorous, a passing thought. She contrasts with these men who have dominated others all their lives and yet are still full of hate and violence.

 While the old man is there, Celie's eyes meet Mr.____'s and there is a moment of understanding between them. Ironically, a situation where the old man is complaining about some harm to Celie is the moment that brings them together. The old man is now powerless. He threatens a little about his land but in his middle age Mr.____ has finally made the stand he should have made years ago. ✪ What do you think has changed Mr.____? ✪ Will he be nicer to Celie now?

LANGUAGE, STYLE, AND STRUCTURE

In this series of letters the major character moves from almost complete incomprehension of what is going on around her to a worldly wisdom beyond her age and experience. It is difficult to believe that the now mature Celie, cynical about the people at the church and aware of life's cruelty, would still maintain this naive correspondence that she knows will never be answered.

Celie's language becomes more lucid and imaginative although she never adopts a formal style of English. Her descriptions of Shug in particular are highly charged, for example, in her description of Shug's naked body or the way Shug preens herself comically in front of Celie, or later the way she refuses to admit she finds Celie's food tempting. Each letter is longer and so are her paragraphs and sentences as the mature Celie's thoughts become less disjointed and more

COMMENTARY

aimed at getting exactly the right tone. The imagery Celie resorts to is often that of her environment: the trees, food, fruit, shades of black and brown.

Another obvious part of the structure of this novel is coincidence and plotting. In earlier sections we saw the coincidence of Celie spotting her daughter six years after she last saw her. As the novel progresses, the coincidences become increasingly obvious. Here the author needs to bring Celie and Shug together, so Shug's illness close to town brings that about. As the story continues, the plot grows in importance; it has to to bring about the happy ending.

Test yourself

- In this novel minor characters appear briefly, take part in some event in Celie's life, and fade away again. Why do you think Alice Walker introduces (a) Mr.____'s father and (b) Tobias at this moment? Make a Mind Map of other such characters and say what their function is in the novel.

- Draw a Mind Map showing Shug's character. Extend the arms of the Mind Map with events from the novel. Another arm could show relevant quotes.

- The story so far has moved from a high level of violence to near-peacefulness as Celie has matured and Shug Avery has come into her life. Each of the characters can be said to illustrate some aspect of violence. Make a bar chart using two different colors to show (a) how violent each character is toward others and (b) how far each is a victim of violence. Are the bars for each character simply opposites of one another, with Mr.____, for example, near the top of one and near the bottom of the other? If not, can you explain why not?

- Now that Shug Avery has arrived, do you think that all Celie's problems are ended? Have any of them ended at all or is this just a lull in the violence of her life? The two women we have encountered so far who are not controlled by men use violence either physically or verbally. Is the moral of the story that violence must be used against violence?

THE COLOR PURPLE

> **?** Look at your Mind Map of Celie's connections and add Shug and Mr.____'s father and brother to it.

Take a break before hearing about Harpo's eating problem.

Letters 28–35

Letter 28

- ◆ Sofia tells Celie about Harpo's eating.
- ◆ Celie observes it for herself.

In the marriage of Harpo and Sofia, Alice Walker is working out her ideas of what happens when a woman fights back against violence. Harpo's violence is particularly stupid because we can see what he is unable to see – he is destroying his own happiness by trying to make Sofia do what he says. It is also comic because he is physically incapable of subduing Sofia.

Sofia complains about Mr.____ to Celie. It is because of him that Harpo is so unhappy. Strangely, Celie has a nearly good word to say for Mr.____. While this isn't love in any sense of the word, we can sense that things might yet work out between Celie and Mr.____ into a form of companionship at least.

Letter 29

- ◆ Celie tries to tell Harpo what he is about to lose.

Celie explains to him that Sofia loves him and will do whatever he wants without being threatened, but what he wants is that sense of power over another human being that he sees his father has. In this ugly male world Harpo cannot see where happiness lies. Celie points out to Harpo that Mr.____'s real love is Shug Avery and Mr.____ has no power over her at all. This seems to bring some comfort to Harpo, and he throws up all the food he has eaten as if he realizes that he no longer needs it.

COMMENTARY

Letter 30

◆ Sofia tells Celie how she feels.

For Sofia, the problem is not one of getting the upper hand in her marriage. Sofia conducts her life the way she sees fit and knows that eventually she will leave Harpo. As she says, he doesn't want a wife; he wants a dog. She tells Celie that she hates him because he can still enjoy sex even though it means nothing to her.

When Celie thinks about sex, all she can compare Sofia's story with is Mr.____ *doing his business*, so she cannot really relate to Sofia's regret at the loss of her sexual pleasure. She briefly thinks about how the thought of Shug aroused her, but says it is like going to the end of a road that turns back on itself, meaning there is no future in that kind of love.

For Celie the troubles between Sofia and Harpo have seemed unresolvable because she has never even considered that Sofia had any option but to stay with him. But Sofia is lucky. She has a sister who can take her in. This to Celie is an amazing luxury and brings her pain at the thought of Nettie still being alive and able to take her in. ✪ Do you think if Celie could leave now, with Shug at Mr.____'s house, she would?

Letter 31

◆ Sofia leaves Harpo.

Sofia's sisters are all big and strong like Sofia. Celie gives Sofia the quilt she had been making for Shug Avery as a sign of her sense of solidarity with Sofia.

Letter 32

◆ Harpo turns his house into a juke joint.

With Sofia gone, Harpo discovers that he is attractive to other women, that he isn't as stupid as Mr.____ has always told him, and that there are ways of making money besides laboring on the land. ✪ Why do you think Alice Walker allows Harpo to be so happy after his wife has left him? Is the moral of this that it is good for men to abandon

THE COLOR PURPLE

their families? ✪ Is this just another twist of the plot to allow Celie to watch Shug sing?

Letter 33

◆ Shug sings at the juke joint and makes it a success.

Respectable women don't visit juke joints. ✪ Is this Mr.____'s real opinion or does he just want to stop Celie from having some fun?

Watching Shug sing to Mr.____ makes Celie sad because of the hopelessness of her love. But then Shug sings the song that Celie inspired. ✪ Celie ignores the lyrics of the song about *some no count man doing her wrong*. Is she right to ignore the words?

Shug begins the process of Celie's liberation here. Mr.____ tries to stop Celie from going to the juke joint and Shug puts that aside with a few well-chosen words.

Letter 34

◆ Celie and Shug talk about Shug leaving and Mr.____ beating Celie.

If this novel is about the many forms that love can take, then one of those forms is the twisted one that Mr.____ experiences. He beats Celie because he loves Shug. The thought that he could beat anyone comes as a complete shock to Shug. ✪ Do you think this will affect Shug's feelings for him?

Letter 35

◆ Celie and Shug talk about sex.

Mr.____ and Shug have rekindled their sexual relationship. They are great lovers, making love for hours and sleeping all day until they go back to the juke joint at night. We realize that it isn't a caring kind of love at all but a purely physical passion. Shug doesn't like Mr.____ much as a person, she says, especially since she has learned about his bullying.

The two women begin to discuss sex, and Shug, who has few inhibitions, describes what enjoying sex is like for a woman.

COMMENTARY

She sends Celie off with a mirror to look at her body and Celie is impressed by what she has seen. She remembers the pleasure of breast-feeding her babies before they were taken away from her. The scene displays talk about love but it is also a loving scene where Celie is enjoying the company of the woman that she loves.

Shug at least has the courtesy to ask Celie if she minds her sleeping with Mr.____. Celie doesn't say what she really feels, that she doesn't mind who he sleeps with, it is Shug's body she is jealous of, not his.

In Mr.____'s eyes Celie is a piece of property, taken in to service his needs. His idea of sex with her is very different from the lovemaking that he enjoys with Shug. Celie describes their sex life as if Mr.____ uses her to relieve himself, rather than as a mutually agreeable activity. The one relief in this miserable description is that at least she no longer describes sex as suffering, but as something at which she is present without taking part.

Time for reflection

? Draw a Mind Map showing the relationship between Celie and Shug. Each arm can represent an aspect of their friendship while further branches can represent illustrations of that. A suggested start appears on page 54. One side of the Mind Map can be the things that Celie does for Shug Avery, and the other side can be things that Shug Avery does for Celie. The Map will need to be added to as the story progresses.

? Most of the themes of the novel are illustrated in the story so far. Draw and cut out pictures of the icons used here and lay them out on a big sheet of paper. Draw lines to connect them. For example, the relationships between men and women are affected by the themes of slavery and freedom, and violence. This last theme has a bearing on the relationships between women and all are connected in some way with love, even violence.

? Mr.____ has become a far more complex character since Shug's arrival. Create a Mind Map for him, showing the contradictions in his character. Do you think bullies can be cured? If Mr.____ is typical of men in this community, how would you describe them? Are there any good men in this story?

? Identify the people or ideas referred to in Celie's images (Answers on p. 93):

1 *like running to the end of the road and it turning back on itself.*
2 *skinny as a bean and her face full of eyes.*
3 *sound low down dirty to me, like what the preacher tell you it a sin to hear.*
4 *like a little mouse been nibbling the biscuit, a rat run off with the ham.*
5 *sick as she is, if a snake cross her path, she kill it.*

Take a break. Listen to some low-down dirty music for a while.

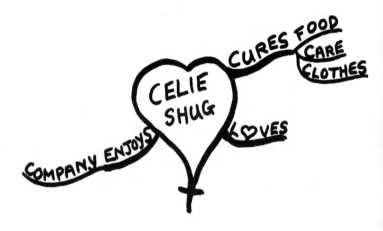

Letters 36–44

Letter 36

◆ Sofia visits the juke joint and punches Mary Agnes.

Sofia turns up with a big man, and Mr.____ at first pretends that he is pleased to see her. Really he is scandalized by

COMMENTARY

her behavior. She has broken every rule in his how-wives-must-behave book. She has a new boyfriend, she has left her children at home, she is drinking in public, all added to the fact that she refused to be beaten by Harpo. But the prizefighter stops Mr.____ from creating an unpleasant scene. All he can do is whisper to her about where her children are, an irony that she immediately picks up since he has made no effort at any time to look after his own children.

Mr.____'s power base is coming to an end. Harpo is happy and independent; his children are gone; Celie is now allowed out to the juke joint; and he has failed to make Sofia's life miserable. The theme of acceptable male and female behavior continues here as Shug tells Sofia how sexy she looks. Celie thinks that Shug is like a man in the way that she talks. ✪ Is she right?

Then the inevitable confrontation between Sofia and Harpo takes place. Harpo behaves in a way that makes us realize he has learned nothing from the failure of his marriage. Sofia and Harpo have gotten over his initial aggression, and they dance. In this scene we see what Shug was probably expecting when she arrived at Celie's house. Squeak challenges Sofia and gets punched in the face. ✪ Celie says that Squeak is like her. What do you think she means? Do you agree? ✪ What would Mr.____ do if someone punched Celie?

Letter 37

◆ Celie relates the story of Sofia and the mayor's wife.

For the first time in this novel the themes are related to the wider American issue of racial prejudice. If Mr.____ denies the rights of the women and children over whom he has power, the white people in this town deny the rights of the blacks – men or women. The black community's values mimic the whites – find someone you can treat badly and who can't fight back. Sofia has dealt with the black men in her life by fighting back, using their tactics to defeat them. But here she comes up against a power that cannot be fought off. There are more of them, and they have guns and the law to protect them.

The mayor's wife sees Sofia with a wristwatch, a car, and well-cared-for children, and decides she wants Sofia for her maid. Sofia is rude to her, the mayor slaps Sofia, Sofia punches the mayor, and the consequences are inevitable. ✪ Could Sofia have done anything to stop this chain of events once the wife had asked her to be her maid?

The way in which Mr.____ persuades the sheriff is interesting. First he reminds the sheriff how closely related he is to Bubba, Mr.____'s son, who is in jail. Then he "Uncle Toms" for a while, exaggerating his black vernacular, and then he appeals to their common burden, the contrariness of women.

Here we have further examples of the way women in this novel help and support one another. Even Squeak, one of Sofia's victims, is terrified for Sofia. Celie immediately does what she can to fix Sofia's injuries. Strangely, even Mr.____ does something to help. It is he who gets Celie into the jail to see Sofia. ✪ Why do you think he does this?

Before she begins to tell Squeak the story of Sofia, Celie asks Squeak what her real name is and advises her to insist on being called by it. ✪ Why does she do this? Is she right?

Letter 38

◆ Mr.____, Celie, and Harpo go to visit Sofia in jail.

Sofia is now a slave who for the next 12 years will live or die at the will of the jailers. She has no rights and has learned to behave like Celie in order to stay alive. Sofia's way of learning to survive has brought her to this situation. It is the lowest point in the novel so far. One of the two independent women has been brought down by the strength that gave her freedom in the first place. Physically crushed, she dreams of murder.

We note also that by now Shug has left Celie. Her leaving went without mention in the letters to God. ✪ Why do you think Walker omits that bit of Celie's life? In the Spielberg movie a scene is inserted where Celie and Mr.____ take Shug to the road to meet a car. Mr.____ and Shug walk along arm in arm and Celie follows, carrying Shug's cases. ✪ How does that scene change Celie's story and why do you think Spielberg included it?

COMMENTARY

Letter 39

◆ Sofia's friends plan her escape.

In the face of white oppression the extended family undertakes to help Sofia. Now, for a time at least, the men and women in this society are on the same side. The plans that each one suggests reveal much about their characters. Harpo plans a breakout, the prizefighter suggests smuggling a weapon into the jail, Celie has a fantasy about God and angels, but it is Mr.____ who comes up with the plan. The warden of the jail is the brother of Squeak's white father. It will be her job to influence the warden.

Celie's vision of escape to freedom for Sofia involves a caricature of a white God in a chariot taking Sofia up to heaven. The angels are completely white and so is God, who looks like a bank manager. The angels play musical instruments and the white God breathes fire and Sofia is freed. ✪ Is Celie being humorous? When she tells the story, why doesn't she say "You" instead of "God?"

Letter 40

◆ Sofia's family gets Squeak ready to visit the warden.

What the family does to Squeak in order to influence the warden is interesting here. Celie tells God that they dress her up like a white woman. Squeak is wearing very respectable clothes, a hat, high heels, and a handbag and Bible. But all these things are slightly shabby. ✪ Why do you think they have chosen to make Squeak look poor?

The story they have concocted for Squeak to tell is a plausible one in the eyes of regular, patriarchal society where women compete for male attention. Squeak will pretend that she hates Sofia and is angry that Sofia isn't being punished enough. She will say that prison to Sofia is a rest from her six children and that what would mortify her more would be if she were forced into being the mayor's wife's maid. In addition, Squeak must make the warden aware, without actually saying it, that he is her uncle. ✪ What would he do if she were to announce their relationship? ✪ Do you think it is their intention that Squeak should make herself sexually available to him?

The underlying assumptions in this letter say much about society in the southern states of America at this time. It is a community where white men have liaisons with black women, and father children by them. Black people are very much aware of their place in this society, of what will make the whites angry, and of what will appease them. Openly saying that the warden is her uncle will insult him, since white people pretend that there are no such liaisons.

Letter 41

◆ Squeak is raped by her uncle.

The reaction of Sofia's family to the rape of Squeak suggests that they had not thought the warden would sink so low as to rape his own niece. The outcome for Sofia of Squeak's visit is not yet known, but Squeak has realized that Celie's advice was important and insists that from now on she be called Mary Agnes. Her sacrifice for Harpo and his wife has raised her status within the group to the point where she can now have her real name recognized.

Celie has already said that Squeak is like her, in that she is passive and does whatever she is told. Now Shug says to her that if she doesn't tell her friends what has happened to her, the only person she can tell will be God. God seems the last one anyone in this community would turn to.

Letter 42

◆ Mary Agnes starts to sing.

Mary Agnes has proved her worth with the sacrifice she made for Sofia and now she is able to realize her true creativity. The song Celie quotes is about Mary Agnes's color. Pale skin must have been highly prized among black people because in a previous letter Squeak asks Harpo if he loves her or just her color.

Letter 43

◆ Celie sits with Sofia as she watches the mayor's children play.

COMMENTARY

Sofia is serving a sentence, but it seems the mayor's wife is also serving one. Sofia spends all her time plotting murder. Celie and Sofia discuss why black people haven't killed off all the whites, who seem too incompetent to survive. We see just how callous Sofia is toward the white people who have made her their slave when the little boy, in a fit of anger at his maid not following his orders, injures himself. Sofia simply observes the child. Ironically, the little girl has become attached to Sofia, but Sofia barely notices her.

Letter 44

◆ Sofia teaches the mayor's wife to drive.

Sofia relates how the white people seem to be angry at the blacks for letting a good system – slavery – collapse. But Sofia despises the whites, saying that they are unlucky and have no skills to do anything. She calls herself a slave, and one of her sons objects to the term, saying she is a captive, not a slave. ✪ What is the distinction between the two terms?

 LANGUAGE, STYLE, AND STRUCTURE

Increasingly, the letters to God have become a narrative that takes no account of who it is written to. At one stage here Celie even talks about God as a third party rather than as "you." Celie includes stories she has not witnessed herself and the reader often forgets that Celie's voice is between us and the story. The long account of Sofia teaching the mayor's wife to drive is entirely in Sofia's words with no comment on Celie's part.

The language often leaves black language patterns behind, using more commonly used tenses and modal forms of verbs, especially when Miss Millie's words are related. Imagery is still quite simple, mostly similes, and from aspects of everyday life. For example, when Celie describes Sofia's humorless laugh, she relates it to the lyrics of a sad song: *It sound like something from a song. The part where everybody done gone home but you.* While this sounds simple, the irony lies in the contrast between the two sentences. The first sounds pleasant – a line from a song – but then we realize that it's a song about loneliness.

THE COLOR PURPLE

Now over to you

- **?** Complete the time chart you started in an earlier section. We know that this sequence of letters covers about five years, since Sofia tells the mayor's wife that she hasn't seen her children for that long.

- **?** Look back at your Mind Map for Sofia's character. Add these events to it, showing how Sofia's story relates to the themes of the novel.

- **?** Find a quotation from this series of letters to illustrate the following statements:

  1 Sofia tries to avoid conflict with people.
  2 White people can be flattered into doing what black people want them to do.
  3 Mr.____ puts aside his feelings toward Sofia when confronted by the injustices of white people.
  4 Sofia frightens Miss Millie.
  5 Because of her newfound self-respect, Mary Agnes develops a talent.
  6 Far from being inwardly subservient to the white people, the black community despises them.
  7 Celie is completely cynical about her religion.
  8 Sofia has learned that the whites want to humiliate and hurt black people.

- **?** Look for some more examples of dialect to add to the list you made earlier of Southern Black English. What do the following expressions mean?

  Clammed, crackers, haul off, preshate, Say what, ast, Uncle Tomming, naw.

Now haul off a while and preshate nature.

COMMENTARY

Letters 45–51

Letter 45

◆ Shug arrives for Christmas with her new husband Grady and a big car.

For their own reasons neither Celie nor Mr.____ appreciates the new husband. He physically disgusts Celie as he puts his arms around her.

Letter 46

◆ Shug explains to Celie why she got married.

Shug has finally gotten over her infatuation with Mr.____. Celie's stories about his laziness and beatings made her see him in a different light. But her attraction to Grady seems even less permanent. Shug is now rich and famous. Her freedom and independence have paid off. Celie talks about her own marriage, which has mellowed into near-respect, with Mr.____ even considering Celie's sexual needs in bed and slapping her only occasionally.

Letter 47

◆ Celie tells Shug about her rape and her children.
◆ Celie and Shug make love.

The only one that Celie could tell about her rape has been God, and since the first few letters, when she was barely able to put it into words, she has never returned to the subject. Now she has someone who loves her and Celie finally has a real person to tell. What seems to have hurt her most wasn't the rape or the brutality but the fact that she never had anyone to love her.

Their lovemaking comes as a surprise to both Celie and Shug. Celie has always believed that her sexual attraction to Shug was an impossible aberration, while Shug has never considered lesbian love before. What they do is an expression of the intensity of their feelings, rather than some conventional and socially acceptable act. ✪ In the Spielberg movie this scene and all the other references to their sexuality is reduced to one chaste kiss. Why do you think he does this? Discuss the question with some friends or bring it up in class.

Letter 48

- ◆ Celie wakes up beside Shug.
- ◆ Shug encourages Mary Agnes to sing.

The feeling Celie has reminds her of the closeness she had with her mother and Nettie but with an added dimension. Celie is now somewhere in her middle thirties and this is the first affection of any kind she has experienced since she was 19 and Nettie left.

For the first time we experience Shug's language reported directly to us. Celie seems to revel in telling God exactly what Shug says. Shug is a free and powerful woman. She has success, all the money she needs, and can say what she likes with authority. She tolerates Grady because it suits her, and she doesn't seem to care much about his spending all her money or making eyes at Mary Agnes. She is enormously generous and helps Mary Agnes to sing. She recognizes, and points out, that singing, dancing, and sex have a lot in common, especially, she says, the way Squeak sings and looks.

Letter 49

- ◆ The text of the first letter from Nettie that Celie has seen.
- ◆ Shug and Celie talk about Nettie.

The two women become more deeply engaged in exchanging their life stories. Shug makes the association between Nettie and the strange letters she has seen Mr.____ keep to himself.

Nettie's letter, which begins this letter to God, is her latest one, stolen from Mr.____'s pocket by Shug in Letter 50. It tells Celie some facts that must excite and tantalize her – that Nettie is alive and is with Celie's daughter and son.

COMMENTARY

Letter 50

- ◆ Shug steals the letter.
- ◆ Celie has a breakdown.
- ◆ Shug tells her about her early life.

Celie and Mr.____ have been getting along for the last few years since Shug's first visit. Mr.____ has helped in Sofia's troubles and Celie's life has been much less difficult. But she cannot believe that he would hide her letters. ✪ Why hasn't he given them to her? Celie told Sofia in an earlier letter that she had never expressed anger in any way and now all her anger seems to take over until, without even being aware of what she is doing, she is standing behind Mr.____ holding his straightedge razor in her hand. Shug gently takes it away and Mr.____ never even notices what nearly happened to him. In the movie this scene is portrayed in a very different way, with Shug running to stop Celie, who might end all her own hopes of happiness with Mr.____'s murder.

When Celie becomes unable to move with the pain she is feeling, Shug puts her into bed and begins to tell her about her own early life. As Celie listens to Shug's confessions she becomes cold and still and unfeeling, and is glad to be so.

If Shug never allowed herself to be treated like Celie, she still suffered for her personal freedom. Her own background was harsh, with a mother who hated physical contact, while Shug, or Lillie as she was named, loved to express her feelings physically. Albert responded to that physical need in Shug. He danced, he made her laugh, and he was a great lover. But he was too afraid of his father to marry her.

Now we learn just how Shug, whom we have seen as a generous, unjealous woman, could have behaved so badly with another woman's husband. She acted out of jealousy and anger at Mr.____ and society, behaving more and more outrageously, despite the fact that Annie Julia, Mr.____'s first wife, was a nice woman and had no husband at home for weeks on end and had no money for food. ✪ Who do you think was more badly behaved – Shug or Mr.____?

THE COLOR PURPLE

Letter 51

◆ Shug and Celie steal Nettie's letters.

A brief letter telling how the two women obtain the key to Mr.____'s trunk and find Nettie's letters. They take the letters out of the envelopes and sort them out to read.

 LANGUAGE, STYLE, AND STRUCTURE

The letters have come far from the first incoherent accounts of Celie's life. She is now reproducing the language patterns of the people that she loves. Mr.____ rarely speaks and neither does Harpo or Grady. When they do, it is often to utter something negative – *I don't know if I want her to sing*, says Harpo about Mary Agnes.

But Sofia's humor is represented in the earlier series of letters, and we can hear her aggressive voice as opposed to Celie's cynical tone. In these letters Shug's voice rings out with its profanities and painful truthfulness.

The imagery is still very simple and occurs at moments when Celie is moved by something. In Letter 48 we have Celie's description of Shug singing: *Sound like Death approaching, angels can't prevent it. It raise the hair on the back of your neck. But it really sound sort of like panthers would sound if they could sing.*

Looking back

? If we are to believe at the end of the novel that Mr.____ is a reformed character, worthy of Celie's friendship, how are we to understand what we have learned about him here? Write a letter to God from Mr.____, explaining why he has been so cruel.

? How far do you agree with the following statements? Find a quotation that supports your view.

1 Mr.____ is a typical cruel man who simply enjoys hurting those he controls.

2 Shug Avery loves to flaunt the rules of society.

COMMENTARY

3 When Celie hears what Shug did to Annie Julia she goes cold and has no more feeling for Shug.

4 Mr.____ has become the vicious man he is through weakness and disappointment.

5 If Grady were to run off with another woman, Shug would be devastated.

? In this story so far Celie has established relationships with very different kinds of people. Match the list of people with one or more of the adjectives that you think best describes their relationship.

Harpo	Nettie
Mr.____	Pa
Sofia	Mary Agnes
Shug	Grady
Mr.____'s children	God

Uninterested, passionate, exploitative, cruel, unnatural, loving, supportive, generous, cooperative, negative, sympathetic, friendly, aloof.

? How would you describe the relationship between Mr.____ and Shug; Mr.____ and Harpo; Mr.____ and his father; Shug and Mary Agnes? For all of these relationships find a quotation that supports your view.

? Go back to your Mind Map of Shug's character and add this new information to it. These letters show the unconventional and cruel side of Shug's nature. Do you approve of her?

Before the next set of letters sit back and imagine the panthers singing.

Letters 52–58

Letter 52

◆ Nettie is attacked by Albert on her way to the town.

The first letter goes back to the day Nettie left Celie's house. Mr.____ follows her and tries to rape her but she escapes and finds the woman Celie told her about. She immediately recognizes Olivia. ✪ How many years ago was this letter written? ✪ How is Nettie's written English different from the young Celie's?

Letter 53

◆ The woman takes Nettie into her home.

The woman Celie met in the street takes Nettie in while she looks for a job. The family, Corinne, Samuel, and their children, treat Nettie as if she were family but she still feels lonely.

Letter 54

◆ Nettie realizes that Mr.____ isn't going to give Celie her letters.
◆ Samuel refuses to help her.
◆ Soon the family will go to Africa and Nettie will have to find a new home.

More details of Nettie's new life. ✪ Why do you think Samuel would refuse to help Nettie get news to her sister? ✪ Is he telling the truth when he says he doesn't know Mr.____?

Letter 55

◆ Nettie goes to Africa as a missionary.
◆ Corrine and Samuel help Nettie to study.
◆ Nettie tells Celie she is with her children.

 Nettie begins to study Africa, where American blacks originated. Nettie tells Celie that black civilizations

COMMENTARY

built great cities thousands of years earlier, that the Egyptians were colored, that the Ethiopia mentioned in the Bible refers to all of Africa, and that it was Africans who sold other Africans into slavery.

✪ How much time do you think has elapsed since Nettie left Celie? In one part of her letter she describes seeing the mayor's wife with a black maid who must be Sofia. Is this possible? Check back against the time charts you have made of Celie's life. She was 19 when she went to Mr.___ and Harpo was 12. At 17 he marries Sofia and at least 5 years later she attacks the mayor. Two years after that she is taken out of jail and sent to the mayor's house. ✪ Is it likely that Nettie stayed for 10 years or more in town without trying to see Celie? There seems to be a real problem with Walker's time frame here. Discuss it with your teacher or friends and see if you can sort it out.

Letter 56

- ◆ Nettie visits New York.
- ◆ She visits black churches and sees middle-class black people.
- ◆ She visits the white missionary society and feels saddened by their attitude.

Nettie's letters are serving to put Celie's story into a wider context. The train journey reveals more about the indignities of the system of segregation that existed in the United States between the world wars. Blacks cannot use the sleeping cars, restaurants, or white people's toilets. A white man sneers at the idea of black people going to Africa. Then Nettie encounters New York black communities and sees people living in relative comfort, with indoor toilets and gas or electric lights.

The difference between the feeling of the black community and the whites is obvious. The whites assist Samuel and his family but believe that they will be of little use in the missionary role, while the blacks think in terms of the help that the missionaries will bring to the Olinka.

Nettie begins to discover that even in the Bible there are misconceptions. Her new church teaches her that all the pictures in her old Bible were inaccurate, that some people in the Bible weren't white: The Ethiopians mentioned are black Africans. This echoes earlier references to God and the angels as white people with God pictured as a bank manager. If God has stayed white in Celie's mind, he may well be changing color in Nettie's.

Letter 57

♦ Nettie goes to England and visits white people and museums.

Nettie's naive tone belies the rather didactic nature of this section of the novel. Walker wishes to make the point of white imperialism being responsible for the enslavement of other countries, and she uses the simple descriptions of Nettie, who only half understands what she is seeing. The white people in England have no idea (yet!) of racism since the England of this time has few racial minorities. Nettie notices that she is allowed to use the same crockery as the white people. She visits the museum and notices the vast treasures (looted – as Walker wants us to realize – by Victorian explorers while Britain's imperialism was destroying the native cultures). But Walker is fair in her apportioning of blame. Nettie is most saddened at the thought of the black civilizations that depended on selling their people to the slave ships.

Nettie appreciates the neatness of England and hopes that a country so organized really could do something of use for the people of Africa. Ironically the next place she mentions is Liberia, where well-intentioned people set up a community of black Americans, buying land from local chiefs and building the capital of Monrovia. It soon lost its missionary ideal and a system of apartheid developed there between blacks of American descent and those who President Tubman and his peers call the "natives."

Letter 58

♦ Nettie describes Liberia and Senegal.

In Senegal Nettie sees African black people for the first time and is amazed at the color of their skin and their bearing. But besides admiring their beauty she finds no sense

COMMENTARY

of rapport with them. They treat her, and perhaps even see her, as if she were one of the white people in the marketplace.

Nettie moves on to describe Monrovia, where one would expect the black Americans who emigrated there to have set up a society without social distinctions. But Nettie just sees more nearly white people in the cabinet and wives who seem disgruntled with their lives. There are none of the "natives" in the cabinet that Tubman talks about. ✪ Is this naiveté on Nettie's part or is she making a political statement about Monrovia's lack of democracy?

A final note on imperialism comes after Nettie's visit to a Dutch-owned cacao plantation in which local "natives" work for little money.

In this letter Walker is placing the themes she has established earlier in the novel in the context of the wider world: Mr.____'s control over Celie, Pa's brutality, Harpo's attempt at mastery, the black society's disapproval of Shug Avery, the white people's rigid control of the blacks in Celie's hometown – all these are part of a wider system of control and power. The rich, powerful nations of the world, she says, use their power to exploit weaker people and gain more wealth. Within their own societies ruling groups wield power over poorer people.

In America this power relationship took on extreme forms: first slavery and then a system of segregation. Sadly, as Nettie is finding out, this goes on regardless of color. She discovers that black Egyptians enslaved the Israelites, black African tribes sold their neighbors into slavery, and black African governments create a class system and agree to foreign exploitation of the poor.

LANGUAGE, STYLE, AND STRUCTURE

After the intensely personal world of one woman, in this series of letters the perspective opens up to the experiences of a naive young girl as she travels across the world with a kind of religious fervor, taking in everything and fitting it into her understanding of the world that until then had been very limited indeed.

THE COLOR PURPLE

While the basic structure of a series of short letters is maintained, the tone and style alters completely. Nettie is more literate than Celie and as she travels and learns, grows ever more so. Her style is a complex mixture of profound reflection and gossip. Letter 56 begins with a description of her newly bought clothes, and moves on to some more serious thoughts on color as represented by white people's Bibles. From there she switches tone again to that of an unsophisticated teenager as she wonders at trains with beds in them, as well as restaurants. Her description of the Harlem of the early twentieth century must be a naive one as she describes the people living in "beauty and dignity." Having come from the poverty of the South, even poor black city people must seem rich to her.

The naive tone continues as Nettie tells Celie what Europeans are, mentions famous white explorers as if they were unknown to her, and wonders at the indoor toilets and gas lighting. The serious, wondering tone of these letters contrasts sharply with Celie's abrupt, cynical humor, which finds something amusing in the harshest cruelty.

Being more literate, Nettie uses fewer specifically black idioms than Celie. She uses the past tense most of the time and has standard subject-verb agreements. Her sentences are longer and she uses quite complex structures and vocabulary, reverting to more homespun language when she chats about clothes or the people she is with.

Over to you

- ? Compare your collections of colloquial Black English with Nettie's English. What differences do you notice? Which colloquialisms does Nettie use?

- ? Do you get a sense of Nettie as a real character yet? Begin a Mind Map for Nettie's character, using information you have drawn from these letters as well as things that Celie has said about her. You could try this exercise as a brainstorming activity with some friends.

- ? Without looking back, try to identify the speaker in these sentences, which are taken from what we have studied so far (Answers on p. 93):

COMMENTARY

1. *They love her. She let 'em do anything they want.*
2. *If you can't tell us, who you gon' tell? God?*
3. *When I don't write to you I feel as bad as I do when I don't pray.*
4. *We and the Africans will be working for a common goal: the uplift of black people everywhere.*
5. *They have the nerve to try to make us think slavery fell through because of us.*
6. *She look so stylish it like the trees all round the house draw themselves up tall for a better look.*
7. *Memphis, Tennessee ain't north, even I know that.*
8. *Gracious God, how'm I gonna tune up my mouth to say all that?*
9. *She seem like a right sweet little thing.*

You could turn this exercise into a game with some other students. Find a piece of dialogue and read it out loud. See if they know who it is.

? Try taking some of the sentences from Nettie's letters and writing them the way Celie would say them. Who do you think shows the most insight so far?

Now take a break. Tune up your mouth for a chat with someone.

Letters 59–67

Letter 59

◆ Shug persuades Celie not to kill Mr.____.

Celie and Shug talk seriously about why Celie shouldn't murder Mr.____. Shug's arguments are purely practical and have nothing to do with Mr.____'s right to stay alive. Celie will become like Sofia and then Nettie will have no sister to come home to. Christ forbore to harm anyone when he could have saved himself from the cross. Killing Mr.____ won't make Celie feel better. But Shug's final and most powerful argument is that she, Shug, will lose Celie if she kills Mr.____.

Letter 60

◆ Celie and Shug discuss how to go on.

Celie feels as if she is dead. She has no sexual desire because she is so angry. Shug suggests that while they wait for Celie's anger to subside they should make Celie some pants to wear.

Letter 61 *(Celie's running on into Nettie's)*

◆ Celie worries that her children might be retarded because of their origins.
◆ Nettie arrives at the Olinka village.
◆ She hears the story of the roofleaf.

When Nettie and her "family" arrive at the village, the Olinka are shocked because they thought all missionaries were childless white people. They also notice the resemblance between Nettie and the children and ask if they are hers. This sets in motion a series of events that leads to the eventual discovery of all the as-yet-unknown facts about Celie and Nettie's parents. It also begins Corrine's jealousy of Nettie, which seems to lead eventually to Corrine's death.

The Olinka welcome the new missionaries and tell them the story of their village. The people there worship the plant from which they make their roofs, since the story goes that without it they all nearly died. Nettie realizes that this is paganism but thinks that the religion of these people somehow seems to suit the place. ○ How does this fit in with the themes of the novel so far? Ask your teacher about this.

Letter 62

◆ Nettie writes about the Olinka women.

None of the girls at the Olinka village are allowed to go to school. Their role in life is to be the wife of an Olinka man and for that they need to know how to cook and sew and look after the house. Knowledge of the outside world would

COMMENTARY

do them harm. Other women who showed a tendency not to conform were sold out of the village to the traders. The women of the village see Nettie as a drudge who has no status in her own society, and no man to protect her. It seems that in this society, too, idyllic as it is in many ways, women are exploited.

The seeds of jealousy sown in Corrine when they first arrived are developing. She tells Nettie she cannot borrow any more of her clothes and that the children are not to call her "Mother."

Nettie's letter ends on a lighter note as she describes her room. She seems to have a great love of the people of this village and their things, so much so that she prefers to decorate her hut with their craftwork rather than pictures of religious figures. It is not overtly stated, but we can assume that this is because these are all white figures and they don't seem right in this black community.

Letter 63

- ◆ Tashi's parents take her away from Olivia.
- ◆ More about the role of Olinka women.

Olivia's friend Tashi is being changed by the things she learns from Olivia. She has become thoughtful and silent and does not seem to take her duties at home "into her soul." Her parents have become afraid that she will change so much that no one will marry her and she will be sent out of the village. We see the missionaries through the Olinkas' eyes for a few minutes. Samuel, Corrine, the children, and Nettie will all die within a few years from the conditions in the village, unless they leave first. They will have no permanent effect on the villagers, whose lives will go on in the same way, regardless of the missionaries and their God.

Nettie sees parallels between her life at home and the behavior of these Olinka women. They do not look the men in the face, just as she and Celie didn't look Pa in the face. The men speak to the women in the same ugly way that Pa spoke to the sisters. She says something here that Celie echoes later in the novel – that the Olinka men listen to the women only long enough to be able to give instructions. A parallel that we can draw

73

ourselves is the way in which the Olinka society expels those women who do not conform to its rules, just as Celie's society drives Shug out or the white community punishes Sofia.

Letter 64

- ◆ A road is being built toward the Olinka village.
- ◆ Corrine's jealousy grows.
- ◆ Nettie describes the Olinka women.

Neither the Olinka nor Nettie are aware of the significance of what they see. The road to them is good because it means that they can travel faster. They first of all welcome the people who will later abuse them. Remember how, at the start of the novel, Celie talks about the Indians who welcomed Columbus into their communities; because they were so good to him he carried them off as booty to Spain.

Nettie talks then about how much the children mean to her and how much she would miss them if they went abroad to school.

In Olinka society, when a woman has had enough male children and her husband dies, she achieves the status of a man; that is, she doesn't have to remarry unless she wants to. Tashi's father dies and her mother Catherine achieves that status. Now that her husband is dead, this woman recognizes the importance of education for her daughter and wishes her to continue to learn.

Like Celie and her friends, these women form a supportive unit, each group of wives being good friends and looking after their co-wives' children equally. They have little or no contact with the men and don't want it. Samuel has problems with this female networking since he believes in monogamy and wishes to teach it to these people. What Walker is suggesting is that even in this male-dominated society, the women have found a system of making things work by cooperation rather than competition.

The women have found that they can manage the men by treating them like children, making sure they have palm wine and sweets. This is the Olinka women's way of dealing with

COMMENTARY

the power of men but it is a dangerous one because these men have the power of life and death over their wives. The blacks in Celie's society deal with the whites in the same way, indulging and flattering them, and like the Olinka women, the American blacks face the danger of these powerful people turning on them. Just as Shug can be accused of being a whore and turned out of her society, these women can be accused of being witches or adulterers and killed.

Letter 65

- ◆ The road is driven through the village.
- ◆ The Olinka land has been bought by foreign planters; the Olinka must pay rent.
- ◆ More girls start to attend the school.

The Olinka's way of life is brought to an abrupt end when the road is completed through their village and they are told that they must pay rent for the use of the land. All along the route of the road, the forest on which these tribal people depend has been destroyed.

Letter 66

- ◆ Corrine accuses Nettie of being the children's mother.
- ◆ The life of the village is gradually disappearing.

Corrine has become ill and finally reveals what she has been thinking all the years they have lived with the Olinka. She thinks that Nettie is the mother of Olivia and Adam and that Samuel is their father. Despite the fact that both Nettie and Samuel swear that this is not the case, she doesn't believe them and won't even have the children near her.

We see the Olinka gradually losing their way of life as first their hunting grounds and then their fields disappear.

Letter 67

- ◆ The truth of Celie and Nettie's early life emerges.

Samuel tells Nettie that he has always believed that the children were hers and that he had taken her in and encouraged her to go to Africa with them out of pity for her.

Then he tells Nettie what he knows of the children's origins. A successful farmer owned a shop that had prospered to the detriment of the white shopowners. One night his business rivals burned down his shop and lynched him and his brothers. His wife was left with two young girls and became mentally ill as a result. She met and married another man, and had many more babies. Two babies were brought to Samuel with the story that their mother couldn't look after them. At this stage of the story Samuel doesn't know that Nettie is one of the two little girls whose story he is telling; he thinks she is a young girl who had an affair with Alphonso and is unrelated to him in any way.

The important fact revealed here is that Olivia and Adam were not incestuously conceived. The news brings an end to this series of letters and allows us to see Celie's response to the news. ○ How do you feel about Alphonso now? Is he not as bad as you first thought?

 LANGUAGE, STYLE, AND STRUCTURE

Nettie's style has moved further away from the colloquial English she first began to write in. Celie has already told us that she cannot make out a lot of the letters because of the unfamiliar vocabulary, and we can add to that the complex sentences Nettie uses. Her style is almost that of a travelogue, interrupted occasionally by personal comments to her sister. Her style is formal and a little didactic and humorless, and stands in sharp contrast to Celie's wild, apparently unstructured writings. Walker seems to be using Nettie to lay out for us some of the things that Celie cannot express and uses the culture of the Olinka and their women to extend and universalize Celie's plight.

Over to you

? Celie and Nettie have grown far apart in their experience of the world, but have they grown apart in the way they understand it? Look at the topics below and suggest what the two women might have to say on each subject. You could try writing what they might say in the style in which they would say it.

COMMENTARY

1. Men 2. God 3. The Church 4. Women's lives 5. Shug 6. Samuel 7. Alphonso.

? Do you find the Olinka realistic? They fit very neatly into what Walker wants to tell us about the role of women. Would the role of Nettie have worked if she had gone to live among a Native American tribe instead? Or among the poor of the inner cities? With other students, brainstorm an account of the Olinka as if you were an anthropologist under the headings: religion; funeral ceremonies; diet; social structure; housing.

Letters 68–72

Letter 68

◆ Celie writes to God for the last time.

This brief letter shows Celie in a state of shock. She responds to Nettie's terrible news of her father's lynching and Alphonso's treachery. Her letter ends *You must be sleep*. She is talking directly to God for once. Shug, too, is shocked at what has happened to her friend and gets the idea for the first time of taking Celie away from all of this.

Letter 69

◆ Celie writes to Nettie about her visit to Pa's.

Coming from anyone else the passage describing the journey over to Pa's house might be oversentimental but from Celie it seems acceptable. The land is different from everywhere else, with an abundance of wildflowers, budding fruit trees, and a beautiful house. ○ Why does Alice Walker make Pa's place so beautiful?

All these years Alphonso has continued in his way of life, marrying first one young girl and then another. He looks young and very happy with a new 15-year-old wife on his arm. This is a man who has learned how to deal with white people.

Celie goes to look for her parents' graves, but there are no headstones for them. She and Shug decide that they are each other's family now.

Letter 70

◆ Nettie tells Samuel and Corrine who the children's parents are.

Here we see what happens when women do not support one another. Corrine has kept Nettie away from her all these years out of jealousy, when just talking to her might have resolved her problems. Her imminent death is related to her jealousy, as if it is this that is killing her, not the disease.

Letter 71

◆ Corrine finally accepts Nettie's story but then dies.

Corrine has deliberately eliminated the memory of Celie because she knew at once that Celie was Olivia's mother. It is the cloth in the patchwork quilt that finally makes her remember. ✪ Does this deathbed scene strike you as particularly tragic?

Letter 72

◆ Corrine is buried.
◆ Engineers come to the village.

Things continue to go downhill at the Olinka village. Nettie describes her life as one of drudgery and loneliness. This letter is about the unpleasantness of the heat and how inappropriate their clothes are. Samuel gives her Corrine's clothes but they are uncomfortable and hot. She also talks about how uncomfortable menstruation is in this climate but calls it her "friend." ✪ Do you think that although Nettie has learned a lot in her travels, she lacks the honesty that life has forced on Shug and Celie?

Corrine's death gets a paragraph, mostly about the funeral rites of the Olinka, but with a brief description of Corrine's sweetness and good intentions. A few more words are expended on her clothes. ✪ Why does Alice Walker kill off Corrine and why does she do it in such an unemotional way?

Time for reflection

? Look at the events that Nettie tells us about and add any new aspects of her character to the Mind Map you have drawn for her.

COMMENTARY

> ? Add Celie's visit to Alphonso to your Mind Map. Has her trip made her stronger?
>
> ? Draw a pie chart of the main characters in the book. Give each a slice of pie corresponding to how much sympathy you feel for them. How do Nettie and Mr.____ compare?

Take a rest. Network with some of your friends for a while.

Letters 73–79

Letter 73

◆ Celie and Shug discuss God.

This is the moment in the novel toward which many of the themes have been working – a statement of intent for the novel as a whole. Celie has undergone a terrible shock when she decided that God, the white man who looks like a bank manager, *trifling, forgitful and lowdown*, was never listening to her. Now she has moved in the opposite direction and decided that there was never anyone there in the first place – that there is no God. Shug, strangely, is shocked by this.

Shug's view of God is much wider than the narrow one Celie has had all these years. To Celie a good, righteous person is someone who goes to church, looks after the preacher, and obeys the rules of society. Shug says she knows she is loved by God and can please God by just admiring his work and being happy.

They both agree that the church was never a place in which to find God, and that many of the people in the church had no real awareness of God. Celie repeats her description of God as an old white man. Then Shug gives her description of God. It is neither male nor female, is inside everyone and everything on the earth, and can be praised by sheer pleasure in the world. Everything, including sex, that gives humans pleasure is praise to Shug's God. The aim of Shug's God and of everything in the world is to be loved. The only blight in all this goodness, says

Shug, is man, who has put himself foremost in everything and even made God in his image.

The "color purple" is mentioned twice in this letter and we know that we are looking at the core of the book's philosophy.
✪ How far do you agree with Shug's philosophy of life?

Letter 74

- ◆ Sofia is finally free of the mayor and his wife.
- ◆ The family discusses Celie and Mary Agnes leaving.

Sofia is free again but she is a different person who sits as if there is no room for her and whose children don't know her. Both Celie and Mary Agnes announce that they are going to Memphis with Shug. Mr.____ behaves as though he still has some control over what Celie does and everyone is amazed when Celie bursts out with everything she has been angry about, telling Mr.____ about Nettie and berating Harpo for the damage he did to Sofia with his need to control her. Celie's outburst revives something in Sofia.

The men's arguments against Celie and Mary Agnes leaving just make the women laugh because they are all finally free of the men and the men haven't noticed anything happening. The anger and blustering of the two men don't stop the evening from ending on a warm note as Sofia promises to look after Mary Agnes's daughter while she is away.

Letter 75

- ◆ Celie curses Mr.____.

Mr.____ seems genuinely hurt that his wife, who has seemed happy for the first time in recent years, should be deserting him now. He resorts to abusing her with outright lies and taunts about her appearance. When he finally learns that she knows about Nettie's letters, his response is to blame her – she, like Nettie all those years ago, has rejected his attempts to be nice to her. Celie's curse calls all her new understanding of God into play. The trees, dust devils, the air itself seems to be helping her curse Mr.____. ✪ Do you think Mr.____ deserves such curses?

COMMENTARY

Letter 76

- ◆ Celie moves into Shug's house.
- ◆ She begins Folkspants.

This is the happiest moment in Celie's life so far as she settles into Shug's house. The story takes on a fairy-tale quality as she describes the house with its childish colors and decorations. Like little girls they sit down together and design a new house, which is round and close to nature. Almost magically, as Celie is freed she develops a skill for making perfect pants. She does it by thinking about the person she is designing for and the designs seem to emerge out of her thoughts. This is testimony to the great power of the imagination both to protect and heal the individual, and to generate creative ideas. Be sure to use it in your own study!

Letter 77

- ◆ Celie considers her language.

We saw that as Nettie grew more educated she lost all her dialect English, but Celie's dialect has remained the same despite her advancing years and experience. One of her employees suggests that people will think she is unintelligent if she continues talking that way. Celie considers the suggestion, tries to talk the new way for a time, and then decides that the way she talks already is fine. ✪ Do you agree with her?

Letter 78

- ◆ Celie goes home to Sofia's mother's funeral.
- ◆ Celie introduces Harpo and Sofia to marijuana.

Sofia and Harpo are still arguing, this time about Sofia's wish to carry her mother's coffin. But Sofia has finished doing what other people want and now acts according to her own wishes once again. Celie has changed so much since she became free that Mr.____ doesn't recognize her as she walks past his house and Harpo seems amazed at her. Her new freedom has introduced her to marijuana, which she uses, she says, to get close to God. We see how far her thinking has freed itself from conventional wisdom when she shocks even Sofia by saying *Lately I feel like me and God make love just fine anyhow.* The three smoke some marijuana and hear the earth humming.

Letter 79

◆ Mr.____ repents.

 At the funeral Mr.____ looks very good. Harpo and Sofia tell Celie that he now works hard, cleans the house himself, and cooks. Sofia tells Celie about Mr.____'s initial breakdown and how Harpo went and helped him through it. He began to recover when he had sent all the rest of Nettie's letters on to Celie. Mr.____ tells Celie about Sofia's daughter Henrietta who is ill and may not recover. He also seems to appreciate that Sofia is someone special. An added happiness is that Harpo's kindness to his father has regenerated Sofia's love for him. In a way Mr.____ has left his own form of slavery behind.

LANGUAGE, STYLE, AND STRUCTURE

In the didactic way of this novel Celie takes on the discussion of language herself and decides that since she is now free and has no reason to care about what anyone else thinks, her language is just as good as anyone else's. When we look at the things Celie has to say we realize that her language is just as complex and subtle as standard English and can express the things she has to say equally well.

When Celie and Shug discuss the nature of God, there is little sense there that the women are searching for ways to express themselves. Their English has exactly the right words for what they need. In standard English this may well have sounded very strange indeed. Similarly, when Celie describes the flowers and birdsong on her way to Alphonso's house, her English blends in perfectly with what she has to say. Standard English may well have sounded cloying.

Structurally, the novel is following the letter-based style but now Celie is writing to a real person. ✪ Do you think her tone has changed since she stopped writing to God?

COMMENTARY

Think about

? Try turning some of the conversation about God between Celie and Shug into standard English. Does it sound as effective?

? Do the same for the passage describing the countryside on the way to Alphonso's house.

? The story has begun to resemble a fairy tale, or a Victorian morality novel with a happy ending. On the chart on page 84 plot the happiness curve for Nettie, Mr.____, Sofia, Harpo, Alphonso, and Shug. Celie's has been done for you. Do all the characters seem to be ending the story happily?

Chill for a while. Read a fairy tale.

Letters 80–81

Letter 80

◆ Nettie goes in search of help for the Olinka.
◆ She and Samuel marry.

The way of life of the Olinka has been destroyed as the roofleaf is plowed under and the villagers are moved to a place with no regular water supply. Samuel and Nettie and the children go back to England to try to raise some support for the Olinka. The Olinka are descending into a twentieth-century form of slavery as their lands are taken and they are told they must pay for their water, houses, and food. In order to retain some of their identity and independence, the Olinka are resorting to the old customs and ritually scarring their faces and practicing the old custom of female circumcision.

On the way they meet a white missionary woman whose story in many ways echoes those of Shug and Celie, although her circumstances were very different. This woman knew wealth beyond their understanding and yet was also not free to do what she wanted. She set herself free by pretending to be a missionary and going to Africa. In many ways her treatment of

THE COLOR PURPLE

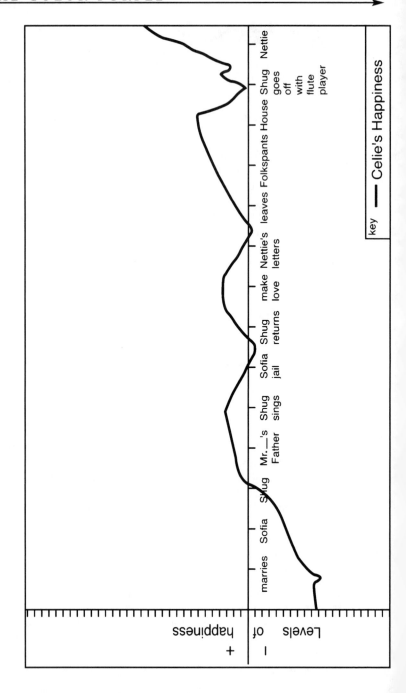

COMMENTARY

the African people with whom she lived was better than that of the black missionaries who arrogantly thought that their God and their ways were superior. She made no effort to change their thinking, only improved their lot physically with schools and a hospital. In that way she and her villagers lived happily together and benefited from each other.

Samuel has grown very bitter about his work with the Olinka. He sees that he has had no effect on their lives, that they have never wanted to be loved by him. For these black American missionaries, going to Africa to improve the lot of the people who they believe sold them into slavery is an act of love, but the Olinka have no interest in the rights and wrongs of slavery. It is what they do. All that Samuel can do for them now is try to improve their physical conditions.

Samuel and Nettie discover their love for one another and Adam realizes that he loves Tashi, the African friend who has stayed behind with the Olinka.

Letter 81

- ◆ Nettie returns to the Olinka.
- ◆ Tashi has undergone the old rites of scarification and circumcision.

Samuel and Nettie have to tell the Olinka that they cannot save them from the modern-day slavery they have fallen into. The Olinka now work in the fields every day to pay for their food and homes. Even the small children have to labor in the fields, so the work of Samuel and Nettie is reduced to nursery education and tending the sick and old. Many of the young run away into the bush to be free of these conditions.

Tashi has undergone the ritual scarring and circumcision in order to please the other tribespeople who see these rituals as a means of asserting their identity. All the children are being mutilated in the same way. ✪ Do you think that scarring is wrong or are the Olinka customs as morally justifiable as Western customs such as confirmation, male circumcision, ear piercing, or plastic surgery?

THE COLOR PURPLE

 ## LANGUAGE, STYLE, AND STRUCTURE

We begin to see that far from being a random series of disconnected letters, the novel has a complex structure. Corrine's death was melodramatic, like a Victorian novel, and also freed Samuel for Nettie's happy ending. What is also fascinating is that although these letters never actually reach their destinations, except many years later in some cases, their issues often mirror events in the two societies they concern. The Olinka are experiencing the same tribulations that their ancestors imposed on those they sold into slavery. The old white missionary lady also had to grab her freedom just as Shug Avery did.

Nettie has finally, to her own surprise, become fulfilled by her love for someone, just as Celie did. Adam's experiences mirror those of Harpo in his efforts to control the actions of the woman he loves. The brutality of Celie's father and Annie Julia's family in disposing of an unwanted daughter mirrors the Olinka's scarring of their unwilling children.

Taking stock

? Look at the scene between Celie and Shug when they first make love and the scene between Nettie and Samuel. Using a Mind Map, trace the parallels between the scenes. Compare it with the one on page 87.

? The story of the old white woman is discussed at some length. Using a Mind Map, brainstorm some reasons why this woman would be included in the story. Perhaps you could make each arm of the Mind Map one of the themes of the novel.

? We have already seen that it is difficult to work out a time scheme for Celie's and Nettie's lives. There are markers in these two letters that suggest an approximate date for Nettie's trip back to England. When do you think this takes place? Look back to the time chart you made earlier and attempt to add the events of Celie's and Nettie's lives to it. How old do you think Nettie is when she marries Samuel?

Take a well-earned break before looking at the next set of letters.

COMMENTARY

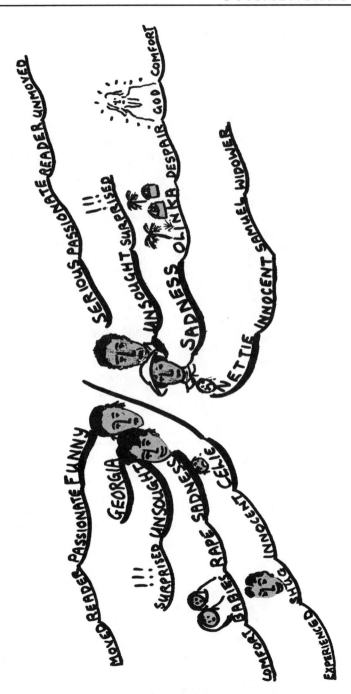

Letters 82–90

Letter 82

◆ Alphonso dies.
◆ Celie gets her house and land.

At first Celie is reluctant to accept anything that has any connection with Alphonso, but Shug persuades her that it is hers by rights and Alphonso was *just a bad odor passing through*. The house turns out to be a grand mansion built by Alphonso after he had made the business profitable. Celie is now free even of Shug's help and can live in complete independence in a beautiful house in fertile, flower-strewn grounds, bigger even than Shug's place. ✪ Why does Alice Walker make Celie's place bigger than Shug's, do you think?

Alphonso has been given a huge monument in the graveyard dedicated to his goodness. He has died happy with a pretty young wife, lots of money, and the good opinion of the community, even the white people. ✪ Do you think this is fair? In a Victorian novel he would get his just punishment and in the fairy tale that this is coming to resemble he would also have something terrible happen to him. ✪ Why do you think Alice Walker writes him out of the story in this way?

Letter 83

◆ Shug tells Celie that she is in love with a teenaged boy (Germaine).

Celie is reduced to the silent, inadequate person she was years ago by this piece of news. All she can do is write down what she feels, but she tells Shug that she cannot stop loving her, whatever Shug does. She gives Shug her freedom.

Letter 84

◆ Henrietta's illness gets worse.
◆ Celie goes to visit Mr.____'s house.

Sofia's youngest child is very ill and it is concern for the child that brings Celie back into Mr.____'s company.

She visits his house and discovers that he has changed completely and this change is figured in his brightly painted, neat house. He has taken to collecting shells, in one of which they can hear the sea. He collects shells because Shug once had one and he does it as an act of love for Shug. He later seems to realize that Celie misses Shug as much as he does and the feeling brings them closer together.

Mr.___ tells Celie that when he first married her she reminded him of a bird, liable to fly away at any moment. He is able to look back at those days and see the mistakes he made and he obviously regrets them. He appreciates Celie now, but she assures him that she feels no attraction to men at all: *Take off they pants, I say, and men look like frogs to me. No matter how you kiss 'em, as far as I'm concern, frogs is what they stay.* Perhaps this is a humorous reference to the fairy-tale nature of this story; this is one fairy tale where the frog stays a frog and doesn't turn into a prince.

Letter 85

◆ News comes that Nettie is dead.

Celie's fairy tale is at a very low point. She has lost her lover and her sister and now all she has is a big empty house and no hope for the future. Living under these circumstances seems hard to bear.

Letter 86

◆ Nettie plans her return home.
◆ Tashi and her mother have run off to the bush.

The conditions of the Olinka are worsening all the time. Their lack of fresh food, especially yams, means that they are susceptible to malaria and other illnesses. Tashi worries that when the children return to America they will be shocked by the racial prejudice, never having experienced it in Africa. When they return they will also be very poor since they have no savings – all their money has gone into supporting the Olinka.

Nettie's view of God has changed radically since arriving in Africa. She now talks about a God that is formless, but exists inside everyone, similar to the God that Celie and Shug have arrived at. Nettie also worries that Celie will be broken by years of abuse by Mr.____ and will not be the sister she left behind 30 years ago.

Letter 87

- ◆ Mr.____ and Celie grow closer.
- ◆ Sofia and Eleanor Jane fall out.
- ◆ Shug visits her son.

Celie has grown very sad on her own in her house and Mr.____ has become good company for her. They talk about old times and Mr.____ now genuinely regrets that he kept her from Nettie and now she will never see her again. Celie notices that he really listens to what she has to say and believes that he is now living a good, natural life.

Thinking about the old times makes Celie remember Sofia's new problems, one of which is the little white girl she brought up at the mayor's house, now a married woman. She remained attached to Sofia even after Sofia was released from service at the mayor's house. Celie recounts a scene where Sofia finally tells Miss Eleanor Jane that the white woman's baby son means nothing to her. The conversation is about race relations in America as much as it is about Sofia and Eleanor Jane.

The two women feel for each other, Eleanor Jane because her parents never loved her, and Sofia because Eleanor Jane made her life at the mayor's house bearable. But they are from different social classes and races and they can never be real friends. Eleanor Jane's son will grow up to be a red-necked racist, and asking Sofia to give affection to a future tormentor is unrealistic.

It is long past the six months that Shug said she needed with Germaine, and Celie has grown resigned to never getting her back. She recognizes that Shug is learning and resolving some of the issues in her life. One of these resolutions is to go and see one of her children, who works as a schoolteacher on a Native American reservation. He, like Nettie, is discounted by the people he tries to help. His love

COMMENTARY

for Shug's parents helps Shug resolve some of her difficulties with their memory.

While Shug talks to her son about her parents, Mr.___ and Celie talk about their love for Shug. They seem to love her for different reasons – Mr.___ because she speaks her mind, is forthright, and like Sofia will fight for what she wants, Celie because they have suffering in common. Both of them agree that they have been lucky to have been loved by Shug Avery.

Celie teaches Mr.___ to sew and as she does so she tells him about an Olinka tribal myth that Nettie has told her, associated with the name Adam. The legends suggest that the Olinka tribe once produced a lot of white children whose mothers they quickly killed and whom they expelled from the village. Once the white children were thrown out of the community they were forgotten, just like the people sold to the slavers because they didn't fit into the community.

To the Olinka the word for white means the same as naked and when they heard the story of Adam and Eve being thrown out of the garden naked, they assumed it was the story of their discarded white children. The Olinka believe that the white people who have come to destroy their village are the children they once expelled and that they will destroy each other and many black people too. It seems almost a prophecy since this is around the time of World War II. ✪ Why does Alice Walker give Celie this story to tell and not include it in one of Nettie's letters?

Letter 88

◆ Nettie leaves the Olinka.

The fairy tale continues as Adam somehow finds Tashi and her mother in the bush and they go on to find a thriving secret community living in a rift valley deep in the jungle with temples, an infirmary, schools, and farms – black people thriving and planning raids against the white exploiters of their continent. Adam and Tashi leave the rift valley and return to the Olinka village, where Adam adopts the scars of the tribe and the two are married. They immediately leave, presumably to join the ship that is sunk by a torpedo.

THE COLOR PURPLE

Letter 89

- ◆ Sofia and Eleanor Jane resolve their differences.
- ◆ Mr.____ explains himself some more.
- ◆ Shug comes home.

With Sofia working in Celie's store, Eleanor Jane has offered to look after Henrietta and prepare the food she needs. Henrietta seems to like Eleanor Jane's baby son and Eleanor Jane has found out why she had Sofia for a maid in the first place. Sofia is happy with the honesty in her relationship with Eleanor Jane now. The two woman can be friends as equals rather than as rich white woman and ex-servant.

Mr.____ begins to explain how the change came about in him. He began to ask the big philosophical questions about life and while he did he began to understand the smaller things. He realized he owed it to his children to try to help them and although that didn't work out, he realizes that Harpo loves him, as do Sofia and her children. Just as Celie has learned that she had to make her own freedom and be independent, even from Shug, Mr.____ realizes that his suffering was his own doing and that, if it cannot be undone, at least he can move on to being a better person.

Suddenly Shug returns. Her fling with the young musician is over and she is even slightly jealous that Celie may now love Mr.____ more than her.

Letter 90

- ◆ Nettie comes home.

Celie's joy is complete as this letter describes the return of her sister and their family from Africa. The story ends with a great family reunion on the Fourth of July, when white Americans celebrate their freedom from the colonial power. This family barbecue is also a celebration of the freedom of all these characters from their unhappy pasts. Even Mary Agnes has appeared from South America, ready to look after her daughter again and having dumped the unsaveable Grady along the way.

COMMENTARY

Over to you

- In one of her last letters Nettie says it has been nearly 30 years since she last saw Celie. Look back to your time chart and see how much of the 30 years you can identify in terms of events in Celie's and Nettie's lives. Add world events to it.

- Look back to the graph showing the happiness rating of each of the characters and add events since Letter 80 to it. Do all of them deserve the happiness they got? Do you find such a happy ending as this acceptable or must we see this story as a kind of fable or fairy tale in order to accept it?

- An important element of this novel is its series of discussions about religion. Describe how each of the following groups or characters understands God. This might be done as a Mind Map. Remember that Celie and Nettie develop their view as the novel progresses.

  Nettie; Celie; Shug; the Olinka; Albert; Samuel; the black community; the white community.

Answers

PAGE 54

(1) Celie's sexual attraction to Shug
(2) Shug
(3) Blues
(4) When Shug secretly eats some of Celie's food
(5) Shug's meanness.

PAGE 70

(1) Harpo
(2) Shug
(3) Nettie
(4) Nettie
(5) Sofia
(6) Celie
(7) Celie
(8) Squeak
(9) Celie.

TOPICS FOR DISCUSSION AND BRAINSTORMING

Generally, reviewers of the novel tend to see its strengths in the immediacy and authenticity of Celie's "folk voice," which avoids the oversentimentality that such a story could encourage as well as keeping the didactic nature of such a book under control. Walker is seen as part didact, part poet.

Many commentators on *The Color Purple* have been feminist critics who have focused on the way in which Walker has used various techniques to convey her views about women. Many concentrate on how the novel treats the estrangement between black men and women. A general criticism of the work is that it reinforces damaging racial stereotypes about black men. Few of the men in the novel have much physical presence, although the same criticism can be made of the novels of Jane Austen, who also writes about women.

Several critics focus on the weakness of the African element in the novel. While the function of these letters is obvious – to extend the theme of exploitation beyond Celie's small world – the overall effect is thought to be little more than monologues on African history.

One train of critical thought about the novel is its absence of a political explanation for the hardships of all these groups of people. While Alice Walker makes the connection between colonialism, racism, and sexism, she resolves the problem in an individual way and avoids confronting the radical feminist idea that patriarchy and capitalism go hand in hand. One could argue that all she does in the novel is promote her favorite characters out of the slave section of society into the capitalist one, leaving all the other people to suffer. Celie becomes an employer, a householder, a matriarchal figure in an extended family that includes her blood relations and those she has adopted along the way. The story ends in a kind of fairy-tale rural Utopia where even the countryside is more beautiful than anywhere else.

A feminist critic, Bell Hooks, sees problems in the novel that relate to the character of Sofia. She acknowledges the novel's

TOPICS FOR DISCUSSION AND BRAINSTORMING

power, which she says cuts across both academic study and popular literature, and appeals regardless of gender, race, and class. But she sees Sofia's tragic fate as a failure of Walker's vision. Celie and Shug succeed, she says, because they never really pose any threat to the structure of society. Capitalism and patriarchy will continue despite the fact that Celie is now happy and fulfilled. Sofia, on the other hand, is a real threat to the system. If black women carry on like that, the structure of this carefully racist society will fall apart. So Sofia is punished for being the only real threat to the nature of things in the novel. By the end of the novel no one can restore Sofia to her old self. Hooks also points out that the rape of Mary Agnes by a *white* man, borne by her in the hope of freeing Sofia, has good consequences, unlike the rapes by *black* men, where the horror and brutality of the rape is stressed. Mary Agnes merely comes home a little disheveled.

Hooks also takes issue with Celie's fashioning of pants, as if the women in this novel, far from becoming more womanly, by putting on trousers, the symbol of male freedom and power, symbolically become men. She calls the spiritual aspect of the novel "a narcissistic new age spiritualism" and says that the book suggests that we can have it all – elimination of sexual exploitation, unlimited access to material well-being, racism tempered by concerned and well-meaning white people, and toleration of sexual deviance. For Hooks the happy endings are pure fantasy, gained without struggle or effort, but the novel as a whole, she says, has moments where "the imagination works to liberate, to challenge, to make the new real and possible."

An area where Hooks approves of the novel is in the concept of motherhood. If mothers have an allegiance to fathers, they have to deny their loyalty to their children. In abandoning their motherhood, Sofia, Shug, and Squeak acknowledge a new and more powerful association – that of sisterhood – where any woman can mother a child regardless of its parentage. This, she says, is truly radical thinking.

Critic Wendy Wall focuses on the structure of the novel itself. She sees the epistolary form as its greatest achievement. At a personal level its episodic nature recreates the fragmentation of Celie's life after her rape and the loss of her children. Each letter is divided by varying periods of time, sometimes five

TOPICS FOR DISCUSSION AND BRAINSTORMING

years or more, and none of the letters are ever received or read in the same time frame in which they are written. Celie becomes framed in little time capsules and rarely has the opportunity to revise or review the events of her life. Celie is a serial trying to turn herself into a whole story.

Celie's letters are a secret, with the secrets folded up inside them and it is significant that Mr.____ keeps Nettie's letters folded up inside his trunk along with his pornography and Shug's underwear. They are erotic objects to him. Far from being a part of an earlier tradition of epistolary writing, Wall sees the book as a new departure for the novel, where the reader becomes a voyeur to a private and intimate confession, and far from experiencing a comfortable engagement with the writer, the readers themselves become violators or intruders on the writer's suffering.

HOW TO GET AN "A" IN ENGLISH LITERATURE

In *all your study, in coursework, and in exams, be aware of the following:*
- **Characterization** – the characters and how we know about them (speech, actions, author description), their relationships, and how they develop.
- **Plot and structure** – story and how it is organized into parts or episodes.
- **Setting and atmosphere** – the changing physical scene and how it reflects the story (for example, a storm reflecting chaos).
- **Style and language** – the author's choice of words, and literary devices such as imagery, and how these reflect the **mood**.
- **Viewpoint** – how the story is told (for example, through an imaginary narrator, or in the third person but through the eyes of one character).
- **Social and historical context** – the author's influences (see Background in this guide).
- **Critical approaches** – different ways in which the text has been, or could be, interpreted.

Develop your ability to:
- Relate **detail** to **broader content, meaning, and style**.
- Show understanding of the author's **intentions, technique, and meaning** (brief and appropriate comparisons with other works by the same author will earn credit).
- Give **personal response and interpretation**, backed up by **examples** and short **quotations**.
- **Evaluate** the author's achievement (how far does the author succeed and why?).

Make sure you:
- Use **paragraphs** and **sentences** correctly.
- Write in an appropriate **register** – formal but not stilted.
- Use short appropriate quotations as **evidence** of your understanding of that part of the text.
- Use **literary terms** correctly to explain how an author achieves effects.

THE EXAM ESSAY

*P*lanning

A literary essay of about 250 to 400 words on a theme or character from *The Color Purple* will challenge your skills as an essay writer as well as fix certain details about the book indelibly upon your memory. It is worth taking some time to plan your essay carefully, and a practical way to do this is to follow the three stages below:

1 Make a **Mind Map** of your ideas on a theme or character suggested. Brainstorm and write down quickly any ideas that pop into your head.
2 Taking ideas from your Mind Map, **organize** them into a simple outline, more a listing of the topics you want to include in the order you wish to present them.
3 Be sure you have a strong **opening paragraph** stating your main idea and giving the title and author of the literary work you will be discussing, as well as a **conclusion** that sums up your main points.

*W*riting and editing

Write your essay carefully, allowing at least five minutes at the end to check for errors of fact as well as for correct spelling, grammar, and punctuation.

*R*emember!

Stick to the thesis you are trying to support and avoid unnecessary plot summary. Always support your ideas with relevant details and quotations from the text.

*M*odel answer and plan

Pay close attention to the wording of the question you choose to answer, and allow Mind Mapping to help you to think creatively and structurally.

Before reading the answer, you might like to do a plan of your own to compare with the example. The numbered points, with comments at the end, show why it's a good answer.

MODEL ANSWER AND ESSAY PLAN

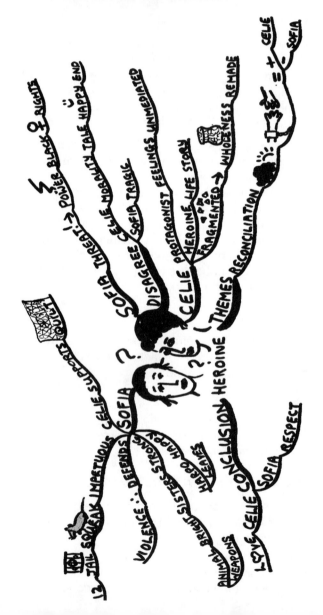

MODEL ANSWER AND ESSAY PLAN

QUESTION
Sofia is the real heroine of this story. Do you agree?

PLAN
- General response to the question showing understanding of its terms.
- Say whether you agree or disagree.
- Put her story into the context of Celie's development.
- Show the ways in which Sofia is indeed a heroine.
- Problematic ending of the story.
- Conclusion, summing up the response to the essay title.

ESSAY

In Alice Walker's *The Color Purple* there are two strong and interesting characters: Sofia and Celie. Sofia, who had been forced to defend herself with physical violence even within her family, also fights to remain proud in spite of the prejudice of white people in the South during changing times. She is imprisoned for 12 years for punching the town's mayor (who had slapped her), but she never loses her pride or sense of purpose and continues to rebel against the social norms. Celie liberates herself gradually and mostly nonviolently from a tragic early life, but is her path to freedom any less heroic?[1]

While it is obvious that the real heroine of the novel is Celie, an interesting case can be made for Sofia as the real radical figure in this novel. Celie is both protagonist and heroine; we identify with her feelings, which are revealed to us in very direct, apparently unmediated bursts. The novel is her life story, and we watch her gradual change as she liberates herself from the fragmentation of her early childhood experiences. But Sofia is a powerful figure, both in Celie's life and in the society that Walker creates, and she represents the real tragedy in this novel. At the end of the novel Celie has re-created herself, but, while Sofia has found some happiness, she never fully recovers from her challenge to the norms of society and its consequences. Celie's recovery is personal; Sofia's tragedy is cultural.[2]

The themes of this novel center around reconciliation, learning, and freeing oneself from the past, and Celie does all of these things. From being an incoherent, fractured child she learns how to become a whole woman and learns to put her past aside and even to forgive those who hurt her. Her one act of violence causes her much pain and she quickly makes amends for it. It occurs when she advises Harpo to beat Sofia, causing herself sleepless nights and Sofia much pain.

Sofia on the other hand has learned to defend herself with violence: "All my life I had to fight. I had to fight my daddy. I had to fight my brothers. I had to fight my cousins and my uncles. A girl child ain't safe in a family of men." Whereas the innocent Celie is raped and has no name for the event, Sofia seems to have grown up knowing that she must defend herself against this.

Sofia is lucky in that she has had the support of equally physically strong sisters who all looked after one another in their perilous home life. She herself is first pictured big and healthy and pregnant marching down the road slightly in front of Harpo. She has bright skin, and ears that prick up like an animal when she is threatened. Even late in life Celie says that "she hold her iron like it is a dangerous weapon." At age 17 she takes on the spite of Mr.____ and brushes it aside, leaving Harpo to follow her or stay behind as he wishes.

Her marriage to Harpo is initially a happy one; she does what she likes and he enjoys the benefits. She works hard in the fields and encourages Harpo in what he does best – cooking and looking after babies.

When things go wrong with Harpo, she doesn't enter into a discussion about whether he has the right to tell her what to do. She defends herself until things get too bad, and then she leaves. This is a truly liberated woman who soon finds a new lover and visits the juke joint to see how Harpo is doing. Like many people who are confident of their strength she avoids conflict but she is impetuous, and when the silly Mary Agnes slaps her face, she knocks her to the ground.

Sofia makes friends with Celie, and the two form a supportive relationship, making a quilt between them, offering help and advice when they can. Sofia admits that she feels sorry for Celie, who has no idea of how to defend herself against Mr.____. She suggests at one stage that Celie should bash Mr.____'s head open.[3]

While the story of Sofia's life is playing out noisily in the background, Celie is learning and beginning to discover her

MODEL ANSWER AND ESSAY PLAN

love for Shug Avery. All her changes are done privately and quietly so that no one even notices them, in contrast to the brash and loud way in which Sofia conducts her life.

The problem with Sofia's life, and to an extent with the novel, is that violence cannot really be allowed to succeed. Sofia can hold her own in the narrow world of her family and will fight any black person who tries to harm her or her children, but, when confronted by the might of the white people, she becomes a victim of her own strength. She punches the mayor of the town and is brutally beaten and spends the next 12 years suffering for her audacity. While Celie follows a path of personal salvation, Sofia takes on the might of corruption and prejudice.

Critics see Sofia as a problematic element in the novel – a failure in Alice Walker's vision – but Sofia actually makes an important point in the novel: The real problems in this society are exploitation and misuse of power, and Sofia is the only person who really challenges those problems.[4] While Celie and Shug Avery never actually pose a threat to this community, Sofia is such a grand, powerful figure that she does. She cannot be allowed to continue in the way she does; otherwise, society will never be the same again. In prison she is reduced to near madness and sits and plots murder every day: "Nothing less than sliding on your belly with your tongue on they boots can even git they attention. I dream of murder, she say, I dream of murder, sleep or wake."

Celie's personal salvation is a result of coincidence, good fortune, and some clever plot twists that negate her incestuous rape, bring her wealth, and reunite her with her family, and it could be said that she really does very little to deserve those things.[5] Sofia stands up for black women's rights not to be patronized and reduced to servitude by the white people, and for that she loses her children, part of her sight, and 12 years of her life. Unlike Celie, Sofia is never freed from her fragmentation by a fairy-tale ending. She never develops a creative talent like Shug, Celie, or Mary Agnes. She ends up working for Celie in her dry goods store, treating customers with contempt and with murder still in her heart: "... she scare that white man. Anybody else colored he try to call 'em auntie or something. First time he try that with Sofia she ast him which colored man his mama sister marry."[6]

THE COLOR PURPLE

There is a partly happy ending for Sofia. She learns to love Harpo again and reconciles herself with the white girl that she brought up, thus extending her world far beyond the cozy rural idyll of Celie and her big house and magically returned family.

So while there really is no case for suggesting that Sofia is the main character in this story, she is certainly a very interesting one. This story is about the way in which women can, through love and caring and mutual support, make their own lives and those of the people around them much better. Celie gains our love with her simple, direct, and often painful thoughts, but Sofia, who uses the same violence as the men, although never to hurt or exploit, gains our respect. Like all great tragic figures people leave her alone for fear that some of her madness will rub off on them.[7]

WHAT'S SO GOOD ABOUT IT?

1. Identifies the significance of the essay question and interprets it. Acknowledges that the statement distorts the point of the novel but has some interesting features.
2. States how the question will be dealt with: showing how Sofia's story is significant.
3. Illustrates some ways in which Sofia is indeed a heroine.
4. Refers to critics as support for the case, and adds personal view.
5. Refers again to the main themes of the novel to set them against the case being made for the interesting nature of Sofia's story.
6. Appropriate use of short quote to illustrate a point.
7. Draws the essay to a conclusion by summing up the response accepting that Sofia is not the heroine in the sense of the protagonist or main character, but she is a heroine in the sense of being a great tragic figure.

GLOSSARY OF LITERARY TERMS

alliteration   the repetition, for effect, of consonant sounds.

allusion   the use of literary, cultural, and historical references.

aside   in drama, a short speech spoken by one character as if thinking aloud, not meant to be heard by others on the stage.

assonance   the repetition, for effect, of vowel sounds.

conceit   extended comparison more notable for cleverness than accuracy.

dialect   regional form of language varying from the standard in vocabulary and grammar.

diction   choice and arrangement of words.

didactic   intended to instruct; in literary criticism, often used in negative sense.

discursive   presenting a logical argument, step by step.

epistolary novel   genre of fiction in which the plot unfolds through letters.

feminist criticism   critical approach developed in the 1960s, based on assessing the role of gender in the production of texts. A particular issue is the subordination of women in a patriarchal society.

free indirect speech   technique of blending a character's words and thoughts with those of the narrator.

genre   type of literary work conforming to certain expectations; for example, tragedy.

gothic novel   genre of fiction popular in the eighteenth century, in which eerie and supernatural events take place in sinister settings.

idiom   a characteristic expression of a language or ***dialect***.

image   a word picture bringing an idea to life by appealing to the senses.

industrial novel   novel dealing with the issues of the Industrial Revolution, often set in the north of England; for example, *North and South* by Elizabeth Gaskell.

irony   a style of writing in which one thing is said and another is meant, used for a variety of effects, such as criticism or ridicule.

magical realism   a fiction style that combines mythical elements, bizarre events, and a strong sense of cultural tradition; for example, *Midnight's Children* by Salman Rushdie.

Marxist criticism   a critical approach that sees literature in relation to class struggle, and assesses the way texts present social realities.

melodrama   sensational drama appealing to the emotions, usually with a happy ending.

metaphor   a compressed *simile* describing something as if it were something else.

narrator   in a novel, a character who tells the story. An *omniscient* narrator has complete knowledge of everything that takes place in the narrative; an *unreliable* narrator is one whose knowledge and judgments are limited and biased.

onomatopoeia   use of words whose sound imitates the thing they describe.

paradox   an apparently contradictory statement that contains some truth; for example, "I hear her hair has turned quite gold from grief" (*The Importance of Being Earnest*).

parody   a copy of a writer's style made for humorous effect.

persona   an assumed identity.

personification   an *image* speaking of something abstract, such as love, death, or sleep, as if it were a person or a god.

picaresque   a type of novel popular in the eighteenth century, featuring the adventures of a wandering rogue; for example, *Tom Jones* by Henry Fielding.

plot   the story; the events that take place and how they are arranged.

GLOSSARY OF LITERARY TERMS

protagonist   a novel's chief character.

satire   literature that humorously exposes and ridicules vice and folly.

simile   an *image* comparing two things similar in some way but different in others, normally using "like" or "as."

standard English   the particular form of English most often used by educated speakers in formal situations.

stream of consciousness   a technique exploring the thought processes and unconscious minds of characters; used by writers such as Virginia Woolf and James Joyce.

structure   the organization of a text; for example, narrative, plot, repeated images, and symbols.

style   the form and expression of a text.

subplot   a subsidiary plot coinciding with the main plot and often reflecting aspects of it.

tense   the form of a verb determining *when* an event takes place.

tone   the mood created by a writer's choice and organization of words; for example, persuasive.

tragedy   a story focusing on a hero whose nobility or achievement we admire, and whose downfall and death through a weakness or error, coupled with fate, wins our sympathy.

viewpoint   the way a narrator approaches the material and the audience.

INDEX

Page references in bold denote major character or theme sections.

Adam 91
Albert (Mr.___) 9–10, 29, 36, 39, 45, 53, 82, 89
Albert's father 47–48
Albert's sisters 36
Alphonso 12–13, 27, 28, 30, 77
Annie Julia 21, 63
Avery, Shug 8–9, 22, 45, 46, 47, 63
Bell Hooks 94–95
black community 44
black dialect 22–23, 60, 70, 81
bonds between women 21, 34, 36, 41, 42, 46, 47, 53, 62, 63, 74, 78, 92
Celie 7–8, 101–104
  appearance 81
  choice of imagery 22, 23, 48, 54, 59, 64
  choice of language 32, 48–49, 81, 82
  duties 45
  selling points as a wife 30, 31
  sense of humor 36, 38
  violent feelings 48, 63, 80
Celie's parents 76
characterization 6
chronology 43, 67, 86, 93
Colombus, Christopher 31
Corinne 34–35, 75, 78
creativity 7

Egyptians 67, 69
Eleanor Jane (mayor's daughter) 90, 92
England 68
epistolary novel 32, 70, 82

fairy tale 89, 91, 94
from ignorance to understanding 18, 27, 30, 36, 44, 45, 47, 58, 63, 66, 68, 80, 81, 91, 92

God 19, 20, 27, 29, 46, 57, 58, 59, 68, 77, 78, 82, 89
Grady 13, 18, 61, 62, 92

Harpo 11, 41, 50
Henrietta, Sofia's daughter 82, 88, 92

imperialism 68

juke joint 52, 54

lesbian love 29, 47, 51, 52, 61, 62
Liberia 68–69
love 20, 29, 30, 35, 39, 40, 45, 47, 50, 51, 52, 61, 74, 77, 85, 88, 90, 92

Mary Agnes 12, 55, 57, 58, 92
mayor's wife 56, 58
melodrama 24, 88
men and women 17–18, 27, 28, 29, 30, 38, 39, 40, 41, 48, 51, 52, 55, 57, 61, 73, 90
Monrovia 68, 69, 80
motherhood 98

Nettie 10–11, 29, 35, 66
  style of her letters 23, 70, 76
Nettie's letters 62, 80
New York 67

Odessa and Jack 13–14, 42
Olinka 2, 19, 20, 72, 74, 75, 77, 78, 83, 85, 91
Olivia 34, 76

Pants 14, 80, 81
plot 4–5, 37–38, 49
prizefighter 57
purple 23–24, 37, 80

racism 10, 35, 55, 67, 90, 94
religion 2, 91
roofleaf 67

Samuel 8, 66, 85
scarring 83, 91
segregation 67, 69
sewing 7, 23
  quilt 41, 51, 78
sheriff 56
slavery and freedom 20, 28, 29, 52, 55, 56, 58, 59, 63, 67, 69, 75, 80, 81, 83, 85, 88, 91
Sofia 10, 40, 51, 90, 94, 101–104
Spielberg, Steven 1, 37
stereotypes 3, 94
  and rape 96

Tashi 73, 74, 85, 91
The Color Purple (movie) 37, 56, 61–62
the spiritual world 19, 27, 29, 45, 46, 57, 58, 67, 72, 73, 74, 77, 78, 83, 85, 89, 90
Tobias, Albert's brother 47, 48
trees 38, 39

Uncle Tomming 56

violence 18–19, 34, 38, 40, 41, 42, 45, 48, 50, 88
Walker, Alice 1
white missionary woman 83, 85